A

Christmas Carol

SPECIAL EDITION

The Charles Dickens Classic

—————— *with* ——————

Christian Insights & Discussion
Questions *for* Groups & Families
by Stephen Skelton

D0168226

Standard®
P U B L I S H I N G
Bringing The Word to Life

Cincinnati, Ohio

Published by Standard Publishing, Cincinnati, Ohio
www.standardpub.com

Printed in: USA
Editor: Laura Derico
Cover design: Brand Navigation
Interior design: Dina Sorn at Ahaa! Design

ISBN 978-0-7847-2391-3

Library of Congress Cataloging-in-Publication Data

Dickens, Charles, 1812-1870.
  [Christmas carol]
  A Christmas carol special edition : the Charles Dickens classic with Christian insights & discussion questions for groups & families / by Stephen Skelton.
     p. cm.
  Includes bibliographical references (p.   ).
  ISBN 978-0-7847-2391-3 (perfect bound)
  1. Scrooge, Ebenezer (Fictitious character)--Fiction. 2. London (England)--Fiction. 3. Poor families--Fiction. 4. Sick children--Fiction. 5. Misers--Fiction. 6. Christmas stories. I. Skelton, Stephen, 1972- II. Title.
  PR4572.C68 2009b
  823'.8--dc22

                              2009023861

14 13 12 11 10 09   2 3 4 5 6 7 8 9

CONTENTS

✦❦ INTRODUCTION ❦✦

> "I have always striven in my writings to express veneration for the life and lessons of our Saviour."
>
> —CHARLES DICKENS, IN A RESPONSE TO THE REV. JOHN M. MAKEHAM,
> WRITTEN ON JUNE 8, 1870, THE DAY BEFORE DICKENS'S DEATH

Jesus often used parables to teach his followers. Parables, fictional stories with spiritual or moral meaning, allow listeners to discover heavenly truth through earthly people, places, and events. Jesus told these stories to link what people already knew, the familiar, with what he wanted them to find, the Father. Through these tales, he taught people—men and women, old and young, rich and poor, believers and doubters—about the attitudes and actions of life in the kingdom of God.

Interestingly, the parable characters Jesus painted, such as the Good Samaritan (Luke 10:30-37), the Lost Son (Luke 15:11-32) or the Unforgiving Servant (Matthew 18:23-35), did not proclaim the gospel message explicitly. And there was nothing holy or especially spiritual about the characters themselves. Indeed, soap operas today often feature similar dramatic narratives. Yet Christ used these inventions to convey gospel truth.

Paul used a similar method to engage his listeners. He employed pop culture references of the time, such as Pagan poetry (Acts 17:28) and unknown gods (Acts 17:22-24), to grab the ears of his audience and communicate Christian teaching. When Paul said, "'Bad company corrupts good character'" (1 Corinthians 15:33), he was quoting a line from a comedic play (the Greek comedy *Thais*, written by Menander). As Paul himself said, "I have become all things to all men so that by all possible means I might save some" (1 Corinthians 9:22).

Many writers and storytellers since have followed the example of Christ in crafting stories that offer more than just entertainment. And though Charles Dickens would not be classified as a "Christian writer" in today's bookshops, it could be argued that he should be. He was in fact a writer who believed in Christ. And as such, his beliefs and his knowledge of the Christian story could not help but find their way into his writings. Indeed, in the quote above from one of his letters, we see this was one of his goals. Throughout his books, you will find Christian values of honesty, compassion, love, justice, and mercy revered. However, perhaps no story he wrote was ever so effective, so influential, in promoting "veneration for the life and lessons of our Saviour" as was *A Christmas Carol*.

Through the study of this work presented in *A Christmas Carol Special Edition*, we will discover the spiritual depth of Dickens and his writing and learn what lessons of Christ are woven in among the scenes of Christmas splendor and the soul-searching of a Scrooge. The accompanying notes to the story are presented to offer insight into some of the biblical allusions and spiritual meanings included in the *Carol*. The notes also offer some help to twenty-first century readers in understanding some of the obscure words and phrases that appear in this presentation of the original, 1843 text of *A Christmas Carol*. Readers may notice unusual use of punctuation and spelling—all of which are original to Dickens's text.

In the discussion questions that follow each stave, or chapter, readers will have the chance to interact with the story and learn more about what Dickens had to say, what Christ says to us today, and what we might want to say in our own lives. The questions were designed in particular so that parents might be able to share the understanding of this story with their children, who most likely have been first exposed to the *Carol* through one of the myriad interpretations of it in film, cartoons, and TV specials, the watching of which has now become part of Christmas tradition in many homes. However, any individual or group of readers can benefit from this interaction with the text, and it is hoped that many lively conversations about Scrooges, spirits, and the true meaning of the season will be inspired by this little book.

As Charles Mackay of the *Morning Chronicle* wrote in his review of *A Christmas Carol*, on its publication, December 19, 1843: "Mr. Dickens here has produced a most appropriate Christmas offering and one which, if properly made use of, may yet we hope, lead to some more valuable result . . . than mere amusement."

I have endeavoured in this Ghostly little book, to raise the Ghost of an Idea, which shall not put my readers out of humour with themselves, with each other, with the season, or with me. May it haunt their houses pleasantly, and no one wish to lay it. [1]

Their faithful Friend and Servant.

C. D.

December, 1843.

[1] In the preface to *Christmas Books* (1852), a collection which contained *A Christmas Carol*, Dickens wrote further about his intentions and intended audience: "My purpose was, in a whimsical kind of masque, which the good humour of the season justified, to awaken some loving and forbearing thoughts, never out of season in a Christian land."

A Christmas Carol [1]

~⚘ STAVE ONE [2] ⚘~

Marley's Ghost

Marley was dead: to begin with. There is no doubt whatever about that. The register of his burial was signed by the clergyman, the clerk, the undertaker, and the chief mourner. Scrooge [3] signed it: and Scrooge's name was good upon 'Change, [4] for anything he chose to put his hand to. Old Marley was as dead as a door-nail.

Mind! I don't mean to say that I know, of my own knowledge, what there is particularly dead about a door-nail. I might have been inclined, myself, to regard a coffin-nail as the deadest piece of ironmongery in the trade. But the wisdom of our ancestors is in the simile; and my unhallowed hands shall not disturb it, or the Country's done for. You will therefore permit me to repeat, emphatically, that Marley was as dead as a door-nail.

Scrooge knew he was dead? Of course he did. How could it be otherwise? Scrooge and he were partners for I don't know how many years. Scrooge was his sole executor, his sole administrator, his sole assign, his sole residuary legatee, his sole friend and sole mourner. And even Scrooge was not so dreadfully cut up by the sad

[1] While today we may use the term *carol* to refer to any Christmastime song, including secular ones such as "Jingle Bells," Dickens is using the meaning of carol familiar to him: a song celebrating the birth of Jesus Christ.

[2] Dickens extends the concept of his book being a carol by calling each chapter a *stave*, a stanza of a song.

[3] The colloquial word *scrooge* means "to squeeze" and is used by Dickens to underscore his main character's primary sin: greed—as in the description of Scrooge as "a squeezing, wrenching, grasping, scraping, clutching, covetous, old sinner!"

[4] His name was "good upon 'Change." This refers to the Royal Exchange, the center of commerce for the City of London. The phrase means Scrooge had good credit, he could be trusted financially.

[5] This is the fourth time in the first four paragraphs that Dickens states Marley is dead. The repetition serves to highlight the death from which Marley makes his miraculous reappearance.

[6] Another bit of foreshadowing—Dickens here refers to the well-known literary figure of the ghost of Hamlet's father, who appears three times in Shakespeare's *Hamlet*.

[7] Dickens was fond of writing about the London landmark Saint Paul's Cathedral, featuring it in many of his works, including *David Copperfield* in which David takes Peggotty to the roof.

[8] Dickens's use of "sinner" reflects the Christian context of his story. You cannot have sin without God to decree sin. Men deal with crime and criminals. God deals with sin and sinners.

[9] *Rime* as used here is a cold mist or fog. The "frosty rime" on Scrooge's head is a description of his grey or white hair.

event, but that he was an excellent man of business on the very day of the funeral, and solemnised it with an undoubted bargain.

The mention of Marley's funeral brings me back to the point I started from. There is no doubt that Marley was dead. [5] This must be distinctly understood, or nothing wonderful can come of the story I am going to relate. If we were not perfectly convinced that Hamlet's Father [6] died before the play began, there would be nothing more remarkable in his taking a stroll at night, in an easterly wind, upon his own ramparts, than there would be in any other middle-aged gentleman rashly turning out after dark in a breezy spot—say Saint Paul's Churchyard [7] for instance—literally to astonish his son's weak mind.

Scrooge never painted out Old Marley's name. There it stood, years afterwards, above the warehouse door: Scrooge and Marley. The firm was known as Scrooge and Marley. Sometimes people new to the business called Scrooge Scrooge, and sometimes Marley, but he answered to both names: it was all the same to him.

Oh! But he was a tight-fisted hand at the grindstone, Scrooge! a squeezing, wrenching, grasping, scraping, clutching, covetous, old sinner! [8] Hard and sharp as flint, from which no steel had ever struck out generous fire; secret, and self-contained, and solitary as an oyster. The cold within him froze his old features, nipped his pointed nose, shrivelled his cheek, stiffened his gait; made his eyes red, his thin lips blue; and spoke out shrewdly in his grating voice. A frosty rime [9] was on his head, and on his eyebrows, and his wiry chin. He carried his own low temperature always about with him; he iced his office in the dog-days; and didn't thaw it one degree at Christmas.

External heat and cold had little influence on Scrooge. No warmth could warm, nor wintry weather chill him. No wind that blew was bitterer than he, no falling snow was more intent upon its purpose, no pelting rain less open to entreaty. Foul weather didn't know where to have him. The heaviest rain, and snow, and hail, and sleet, could boast of the advantage over him in only one respect. They often "came down" handsomely, and Scrooge never did. [10]

Nobody ever stopped him in the street to say, with gladsome looks, "My dear Scrooge, how are you? When will you come to see me?" No beggars implored him to bestow a trifle, no children asked him what it was o'clock, no man or woman ever once in all his life inquired the way to such and such a place, of Scrooge. Even the blindmen's dogs appeared to know him; and when they saw him coming on, would tug their owners into doorways and up courts; and then would wag their tails as though they said, "No eye at all is better than an evil eye, [11] dark master!"

But what did Scrooge care? It was the very thing he liked. To edge his way along the crowded paths of life, warning all human sympathy to keep its distance, was what the knowing ones call "nuts" [12] to Scrooge.

Once upon a time—of all the good days in the year, on Christmas Eve—old Scrooge sat busy in his counting-house. It was cold, bleak, biting weather: foggy withal: and he could hear the people in the court outside go wheezing up and down, beating their hands upon their breasts, and stamping their feet upon the pavement-stones to warm them. The city clocks had only just gone three, but it was quite dark already: it had not been light all day: and candles were flaring in the windows of the neighbouring offices,

[10] Dickens makes a cutting pun with the phrase "came down." When weather "came down," it fell heavily. But the phrase was also used as a slang term to refer to people laying out money, as to give to the poor. When men "came down," they gave generously. But "Scrooge never did."

[11] The superstition of the "evil eye" holds that a person can harm others with a look. In Stave Two, Dickens appropriates this superstitious idea to make a moral point: "There was an eager, greedy, restless motion in the eye, which showed the passion [Gain] that had taken root, and where the shadow of the growing tree would fall."

[12] We often use the word *nuts* today as an expression when something goes wrong, or to refer to someone being crazy. But here the word is used in an older form, suggesting something that created enthusiasm, or meaning favorable or of good fortune, good luck.

like ruddy smears upon the palpable brown air. The fog came pouring in at every chink and key-hole, and was so dense without, that although the court was of the narrowest, the houses opposite were mere phantoms. To see the dingy cloud come drooping down, obscuring everything, one might have thought that Nature lived hard by, and was brewing on a large scale.

The door of Scrooge's counting-house was open that he might keep his eye upon his clerk, who in a dismal little cell beyond, a sort of tank, was copying letters. Scrooge had a very small fire, but the clerk's fire was so very much smaller that it looked like one coal. But he couldn't replenish it, for Scrooge kept the coal-box in his own room; and so surely as the clerk came in with the shovel, the master predicted that it would be necessary for them to part. Wherefore the clerk put on his white comforter, [13] and tried to warm himself at the candle; in which effort, not being a man of a strong imagination, he failed.

"A merry Christmas, uncle! God save you!" [14] cried a cheerful voice. It was the voice of Scrooge's nephew, who came upon him so quickly that this was the first intimation he had of his approach.

"Bah!" said Scrooge, "Humbug!" [15]

He had so heated himself with rapid walking in the fog and frost, this nephew of Scrooge's, [16] that he was all in a glow; his face was ruddy and handsome; his eyes sparkled, and his breath smoked again.

"Christmas a humbug, uncle!" said Scrooge's nephew. "You don't mean that, I am sure."

"I do," said Scrooge. "Merry Christmas! What right have you to be merry? What reason have you to be merry? You're poor enough."

[13] The clerk's "comforter" is his long knit scarf.

[14] Ironically, when the book was performed as a play, this line, "God save you," as well as the more famous line, "God bless us every one," could not be spoken on the London stage, so cautious was the Lord Chamberlain's examiner of plays who checked scripts for blasphemy.

[15] Scrooge's now famous interjection was a common term for nonsense. It seems a familiar response of his in this first stave. However, this will be the last chapter in which we hear him utter it, and by the end of Stave One he can't even finish the word, indicating change already beginning to occur in his perceptions.

[16] Charles Kent, a friend of Dickens, commented, "this description of Scrooge's Nephew was, quite unconsciously but most accurately, in every word of it, a literal description of [Charles Dickens] himself" (*Charles Dickens as a Reader*, 1872).

"Come, then," returned the nephew gaily. "What right have you to be dismal? What reason have you to be morose? You're rich enough."

Scrooge having no better answer ready on the spur of the moment, said, "Bah!" again; and followed it up with "Humbug."

"Don't be cross, uncle," said the nephew.

"What else can I be," returned the uncle, "when I live in such a world of fools as this? Merry Christmas! Out upon merry Christmas! What's Christmas time to you but a time for paying bills without money; a time for finding yourself a year older, and not an hour richer; a time for balancing your books and having every item in 'em through a round dozen of months presented dead against you? If I could work my will," said Scrooge, indignantly, "every idiot who goes about with 'Merry Christmas' on his lips, should be boiled with his own pudding, and buried with a stake of holly through his heart. [17] He should!"

"Uncle!" pleaded the nephew.

"Nephew!" returned the uncle sternly, "keep Christmas in your own way, and let me keep it in mine."

"Keep it!" repeated Scrooge's nephew. "But you don't keep it."

"Let me leave it alone, then," said Scrooge. "Much good may it do you! Much good it has ever done you!"

"There are many things from which I might have derived good, by which I have not profited, I dare say," returned the nephew: "Christmas among the rest. But I am sure I have always thought of Christmas time, when it has come round—apart from the veneration due to its sacred name and origin, if anything belonging to it can be apart from that [18]—as a good time: a kind, forgiving, charitable, pleasant time: the only

[17] Some medieval customs dictated that murderers should be buried with a stake driven through the heart, as is also the legendary method for killing vampires. This furious outburst from Scrooge shows us his distaste for Christmas is so strong, he considers those who promote the holiday as good as murderers.

[18] Dickens speaks with his own voice through Scrooge's nephew as he begins to espouse what Dickens would forever after call the "Carol Philosophy."

[19] In public readings of *Carol*, Dickens changed the passive "fellow-passengers" to the more active "fellow-travellers" to better indicate a living brotherhood among people on the same path.

time I know of, in the long calendar of the year, when men and women seem by one consent to open their shut-up hearts freely, and to think of people below them as if they really were fellow-passengers [19] to the grave, and not another race of creatures bound on other journeys. And therefore, uncle, though it has never put a scrap of gold or silver in my pocket, I believe that it *has* done me good, and *will* do me good; and I say, God bless it!"

The clerk in the tank involuntarily applauded: becoming immediately sensible of the impropriety, he poked the fire, and extinguished the last frail spark for ever.

"Let me hear another sound from *you*," said Scrooge, "and you'll keep your Christmas by losing your situation! You're quite a powerful speaker, sir," he added, turning to his nephew. "I wonder you don't go into Parliament."

"Don't be angry, uncle. Come! Dine with us to-morrow."

[20] While Dickens leaves out the complete phrase, "he would see him [damned or in hell first]," the reader of the day was expected to know it—and thereby understand most explicitly Scrooge's devilish disposition at the beginning.

[21] Scrooge disapproves of his nephew's marrying because—as was also proposed by certain social economists with whom Dickens disagreed—Scrooge thinks his nephew does not have the money for a family and so should not have married, underlining an emphasis on money over love.

Scrooge said that he would see him [20]—yes, indeed he did. He went the whole length of the expression, and said that he would see him in that extremity first.

"But why?" cried Scrooge's nephew. "Why?"

"Why did you get married?" [21] said Scrooge.

"Because I fell in love."

"Because you fell in love!" growled Scrooge, as if that were the only one thing in the world more ridiculous than a merry Christmas. "Good afternoon!"

"Nay, uncle, but you never came to see me before that happened. Why give it as a reason for not coming now?"

"Good afternoon," said Scrooge.

"I want nothing from you; I ask nothing of you; why cannot we be friends?"

"Good afternoon," said Scrooge.

"I am sorry, with all my heart, to find you so resolute. We have never had any quarrel, to which I have been a party. But I have made the trial in homage to Christmas, and I'll keep my Christmas humour to the last. So A Merry Christmas, uncle!"

"Good afternoon!" said Scrooge.

"And A Happy New Year!"

"Good afternoon!" said Scrooge.

His nephew left the room without an angry word, notwithstanding. He stopped at the outer door to bestow the greetings of the season on the clerk, who, cold as he was, was warmer than Scrooge; for he returned them cordially.

"There's another fellow," muttered Scrooge; who overheard him: "my clerk, with fifteen shillings a week, [22] and a wife and family, talking about a merry Christmas. I'll retire to Bedlam."

This lunatic, in letting Scrooge's nephew out, had let two other people in. They were portly gentlemen, pleasant to behold, and now stood, with their hats off, in Scrooge's office. They had books and papers in their hands, and bowed to him.

"Scrooge and Marley's, I believe," said one of the gentlemen, referring to his list. "Have I the pleasure of addressing Mr. Scrooge, or Mr. Marley?"

"Mr. Marley has been dead these seven years," [23] Scrooge replied. "He died seven years ago, this very night." [24]

"We have no doubt his liberality is well represented by his surviving partner," said the gentleman, presenting his credentials.

It certainly was; for they had been two kindred spirits. At the ominous word "liberality," Scrooge frowned, and shook his head, and handed the credentials back.

[22] "Fifteen shillings a week" was the amount Dickens received as an office boy. While fine for a teenage boy, the pay was much too little for a family man. Scrooge knows it—and yet does nothing about it.

[23] Originally, Dickens wrote that Marley died "ten years ago, this very day" before changing it to the more resonant "seven years ago, this very night." In the Bible, seven is a holy number that symbolizes completeness. In *Carol*, the number seven is mentioned seven times in connection to the death of Marley, the worldly miser turned divine messenger.

[24] Although the author's exact intent here is unknown, it could be suggested that, since Marley died on Christmas Eve, and Christ was born on Christmas Day, symbolically, Marley never knew Christ. Marley himself will allude to his failure to follow Christ in his exchange with Scrooge momentarily.

[25] Dickens invokes "Christian cheer" in contrast to the prisons, Union workhouses, Treadmill, and Poor Law—all of which Dickens, one of the most vocal critics of the inhumane institutions of his day, considered very un-Christian. The Poor Law Amendment Act of 1834 took the care of the poor out of the hands of the parishes, which had been required to take food, clothing, and financial assistance to the poor where they were, and made it mandatory that anyone needing aid must live in the government-run workhouses.

[26] We are introduced here to the specter of Want, which Dickens will embody in the wretched character of a girl by that name later on in the story. When she appears, Want is accompanied by a boy named Ignorance. A few lines down from this mention of Want being "keenly felt," we see Scrooge claiming to be ignorant of the desperate plight of the poor, saying "It's not my business."

"At this festive season of the year, Mr. Scrooge," said the gentleman, taking up a pen, "it is more than usually desirable that we should make some slight provision for the poor and destitute, who suffer greatly at the present time. Many thousands are in want of common necessaries; hundreds of thousands are in want of common comforts, sir."

"Are there no prisons?" asked Scrooge.

"Plenty of prisons," said the gentleman, laying down the pen again.

"And the Union workhouses?" demanded Scrooge. "Are they still in operation?"

"They are. Still," returned the gentleman, "I wish I could say they were not."

"The Treadmill and the Poor Law are in full vigour, then?" said Scrooge.

"Both very busy, sir."

"Oh! I was afraid, from what you said at first, that something had occurred to stop them in their useful course," said Scrooge. "I'm very glad to hear it."

"Under the impression that they scarcely furnish Christian cheer [25] of mind or body to the multitude," returned the gentleman, "a few of us are endeavouring to raise a fund to buy the Poor some meat and drink, and means of warmth. We choose this time, because it is a time, of all others, when Want is keenly felt, and Abundance rejoices. [26] What shall I put you down for?"

"Nothing!" Scrooge replied.

"You wish to be anonymous?"

"I wish to be left alone," said Scrooge. "Since you ask me what I wish, gentlemen, that is my answer. I don't make merry myself at Christmas and I can't afford to make idle people merry. I help to support the establishments I have mentioned: they cost enough: and those who are badly off must go there."

"Many can't go there; and many would rather die."

"If they would rather die," said Scrooge, "they had better do it, and decrease the surplus population. [27] Besides—excuse me—I don't know that."

"But you might know it," observed the gentleman.

"It's not my business," Scrooge returned. "It's enough for a man to understand his own business, and not to interfere with other people's. Mine occupies me constantly. Good afternoon, gentlemen!"

Seeing clearly that it would be useless to pursue their point, the gentlemen withdrew. Scrooge resumed his labours with an improved opinion of himself, and in a more facetious temper than was usual with him.

Meanwhile the fog and darkness thickened so, that people ran about with flaring links, [28] proffering their services to go before horses in carriages, and conduct them on their way. The ancient tower of a church, [29] whose gruff old bell was always peeping slily down at Scrooge out of a Gothic window in the wall, became invisible, and struck the hours and quarters in the clouds, with tremulous vibrations afterwards as if its teeth were chattering in its frozen head up there. The cold became intense. In the main street, at the corner of the court, some labourers were repairing the gas-pipes, and had lighted a great fire in a brazier, [30] round which a party of ragged men and boys were gathered: warming their hands and winking their eyes before the blaze in rapture. The water-plug being left in solitude, its overflowings sullenly congealed, and turned to misanthropic ice. The brightness of the shops where holly sprigs and berries crackled in the lamp-heat of the windows, made pale faces ruddy as they passed. Poul-

[27] This reference to the "surplus population" was a swipe at the political economists Dickens despised, such as Thomas Maltus and Adam Smith, whom he felt conveyed the general opinion that the poor had no business being born. This contrasts sharply with the biblical message: "Rich and poor have this in common: The LORD is the Maker of them all" (Proverbs 22:2).

[28] *Flaring links* were hand-carried torches.

[29] The second church Dickens cites is thought to be one of three actual churches: St. Dunstan's (a saint noted below), St. Mary Aldermary or St. Michael's Church (the former two sites mentioned by E. Beresford Chancellor, *The London of Charles Dickens*, 1924; the latter site noted by Frank S. Johnson, "About 'A Christmas Carol,'" *The Dickensian*, Winter 1931–32).

[30] A *brazier* is a large, flat pan used to hold burning coals—a kind of makeshift heater.

terers' and grocers' trades became a splendid joke: a glorious pageant, with which it was next to impossible to believe that such dull principles as bargain and sale had anything to do. The Lord Mayor, in the stronghold of the mighty Mansion House, gave orders to his fifty cooks and butlers to keep Christmas as a Lord Mayor's household should; [31] and even the little tailor, whom he had fined five shillings on the previous Monday for being drunk and blood-thirsty in the streets, stirred up to-morrow's pudding in his garret, while his lean wife and the baby sallied out to buy the beef.

Foggier yet, and colder! Piercing, searching, biting cold. If the good Saint Dunstan [32] had but nipped the Evil Spirit's nose with a touch of such weather as that, instead of using his familiar weapons, then indeed he would have roared to lusty purpose. The owner of one scant young nose, gnawed and mumbled by the hungry cold as bones are gnawed by dogs, stooped down at Scrooge's keyhole to regale him with a Christmas carol: but at the first sound of—

"God bless you [33] merry gentleman!
May nothing you dismay!"

Scrooge seized the ruler with such energy of action, that the singer fled in terror, [34] leaving the keyhole to the fog and even more congenial frost.

At length the hour of shutting up the counting-house arrived. With an ill-will Scrooge dismounted from his stool, and tacitly admitted the fact to the expectant clerk in the Tank, who instantly snuffed his candle out, and put on his hat.

"You'll want all day to-morrow, I suppose?" said Scrooge.

[31] The scene at the Mansion House, the residence of the Lord Mayor of London, was witnessed by Dickens himself as a child, when, lost, alone and hungry, he spied in the window at the chefs preparing one of the Mayor's dinners—until one of the cooks unkindly chased him away (as told by Charles Dickens in "Gone Astray," *Household Words*, August 31, 1853).

[32] One of Dickens's favorite saints, Saint Dunstan (924-988), was an English monk, blacksmith (among other trades), and eventual archbishop of Canterbury, who told tales of being visited by mischievous spirits, one of which he caught by the nose with his red-hot pincers. His mention here foreshadows Scrooge being visited by spirits.

[33] Dickens changed the first line of this famous song—the original lyrics read "God rest you;" in *Carol*, the singer exults "God bless you."

[34] Significantly, Scrooge never lets the caroler get to the lines: "Remember Christ our Savior was born on Christmas Day; To save us all from Satan's power when we were gone astray."

"If quite convenient, Sir."

"It's not convenient," said Scrooge, "and it's not fair. If I was to stop half-a-crown for it, you'd think yourself ill-used, I'll be bound?"

The clerk smiled faintly.

"And yet," said Scrooge, "you don't think *me* ill-used, when I pay a day's wages for no work."

The clerk observed that it was only once a year.

"A poor excuse for picking a man's pocket every twenty-fifth of December!" [35] said Scrooge, buttoning his great-coat to the chin. "But I suppose you must have the whole day. Be here all the earlier next morning!"

The clerk promised that he would; and Scrooge walked out with a growl. The office was closed in a twinkling, and the clerk, with the long ends of his white comforter dangling below his waist (for he boasted no great-coat), went down a slide on Cornhill, at the end of a lane of boys, twenty times, in honour of its being Christmas-eve, and then ran home to Camden Town as hard as he could pelt, to play at blindman's-buff.

Scrooge took his melancholy dinner in his usual melancholy tavern; and having read all the newspapers, and beguiled the rest of the evening with his banker's-book, went home to bed. He lived in chambers which had once belonged to his deceased partner. They were a gloomy suite of rooms, in a lowering pile of building up a yard, where it had so little business to be, that one could scarcely help fancying it must have run there when it was a young house, playing at hide-and-seek with other houses, and have forgotten the way out again. It was old enough now, and dreary enough, for nobody lived in it but Scrooge, the other rooms being all let out as offices. The yard was so dark that even Scrooge,

[35] Here, Scrooge cannot even bring himself to say the name "Christmas," choosing the more awkward "twenty-fifth of December," and refusing to recognize, as his nephew recently said, "the veneration due to its sacred name and origin."

who knew its every stone, was fain to grope with his hands. The fog and frost so hung about the black old gateway of the house, that it seemed as if the Genius of the Weather [36] sat in mournful meditation on the threshold.

Now, it is a fact, that there was nothing at all particular about the knocker on the door, except that it was very large. It is also a fact, that Scrooge had seen it night and morning during his whole residence in that place; also that Scrooge had as little of what is called fancy about him as any man in the City of London, even including—which is a bold word—the corporation, aldermen, and livery. Let it also be borne in mind that Scrooge had not bestowed one thought on Marley, since his last mention of his seven-years' dead partner that afternoon. And then let any man explain to me, if he can, how it happened that Scrooge, having his key in the lock of the door, saw in the knocker, without its undergoing any intermediate process of change: not a knocker, but Marley's face.

Marley's face. It was not in impenetrable shadow as the other objects in the yard were, but had a dismal light about it, like a bad lobster in a dark cellar. [37] It was not angry or ferocious, but looked at Scrooge as Marley used to look: with ghostly spectacles turned up upon its ghostly forehead. The hair was curiously stirred, as if by breath or hot-air; and though the eyes were wide open, they were perfectly motionless. That, and its livid colour, made it horrible; but its horror seemed to be in spite of the face and beyond its control, rather than a part of its own expression.

As Scrooge looked fixedly at this phenomenon, it was a knocker again.

To say that he was not startled, or that his blood was not conscious of a terrible sensation to which it had been a stranger from infancy, would be untrue. But he put his hand upon the key he had relinquished, turned it sturdily, walked in, and lighted his candle.

He *did* pause, with a moment's irresolution, before he shut the door; and he *did* look cautiously behind it first, as if he half-expected to be terrified with the sight of Marley's pigtail sticking out into the hall. But there was nothing on the back of the door, except the screws and nuts that held the knocker on; so he said "Pooh, pooh!" and closed it with a bang.

The sound resounded through the house like thunder. Every room above, and every cask in the wine-merchant's cellars below, appeared to have a separate peal of echoes of its own. Scrooge was not a man to be frightened by echoes. He fastened the door, and walked across the hall, and up the stairs: slowly too: trimming his candle as he went.

You may talk vaguely about driving a coach-and-six up a good old flight of stairs, or through a bad young Act of Parliament; [38] but I mean to say you might have got a hearse up that staircase, and taken it broadwise, with the splinter-bar towards the wall, and the door towards the balustrades: and done it easy. There was plenty of width for that, and room to spare; which is perhaps the reason why Scrooge thought he saw a locomotive hearse going on before him in the gloom. [39] Half-a-dozen gas-lamps out of the street wouldn't have lighted the entry too well, so you may suppose that it was pretty dark with Scrooge's dip. [40]

Up Scrooge went, not caring a button for that: darkness is cheap, and Scrooge liked it. [41] But before he shut his heavy door, he walked through his rooms to see that all was right. He had just enough recollection of the face to desire to do that.

[38] Dickens here is alluding to the often loose wording of Acts of Parliament at the time, which allowed opportunities for the accused to avoid being prosecuted. Daniel O'Connell, an Irish orator, once claimed that he could "drive a coach and six through any act of Parliament" (from *Short Sayings of Great Men*, edited by Samuel Arthur Bent, 1882).

[39] Dickens gives Scrooge one more reminder of how life on earth ends—before the old miser sees how it continues in the next life, at least for those like poor Marley.

[40] Scrooge's *dip* is his candle. The word refers to the process of dipping the wick in wax to form the candle.

[41] Dickens here echoes the biblical teaching that the way of darkness, or sin, often appears to be the easier, less costly way. "For wide is the gate and broad is the road that leads to destruction, and many enter through it" (Matthew 7:13).

Sitting room, bed-room, lumber-room. All as they should be. Nobody under the table, nobody under the sofa; a small fire in the grate; spoon and basin ready; and the little saucepan of gruel (Scrooge had a cold in his head) upon the hob. Nobody under the bed; nobody in the closet; nobody in his dressing-gown, which was hanging up in a suspicious attitude against the wall. Lumber-room as usual. Old fire-guard, old shoes, two fish-baskets, washing-stand on three legs, and a poker.

Quite satisfied, he closed his door, and locked himself in; double-locked himself in, which was not his custom. Thus secured against surprise, he took off his cravat; put on his dressing-gown and slippers, and his night-cap; and sat down before the fire to take his gruel.

It was a very low fire indeed; nothing on such a bitter night. He was obliged to sit close to it, and brood over it, before he could extract the least sensation of warmth from such a handful of fuel. The fire-place was an old one, built by some Dutch merchant long ago, and paved all round with quaint Dutch tiles, designed to illustrate the Scriptures. [42] There were Cains and Abels; Pharaoh's daughters, Queens of Sheba, Angelic messengers descending through the air on clouds like feather-beds, Abrahams, Belshazzars, Apostles putting off to sea in butter-boats, hundreds of figures, to attract his thoughts; and yet that face of Marley, seven years dead, came like the ancient Prophet's rod, and swallowed up the whole. [43] If each smooth tile had been a blank at first, with power to shape some picture on its surface from the disjointed fragments of his thoughts, there would have been a copy of old Marley's head on every one.

"Humbug!" said Scrooge; and walked across the room.

[42] As a child, Dickens lived in a house with a fireplace featuring Dutch tiles with scriptural scenes. In *Carol*, the tile scenes come mostly from the Old Testament: Cain and Abel, Genesis 4; Pharaoh's daughter, Exodus 2; the Queen of Sheba, 1 Kings 10 and 2 Chronicles 9; Abraham, Genesis 11–25 (mainly); and Belshazzar, Daniel 5–8.

[43] Dickens makes a biblical reference to Exodus 7:8-12, which details how Aaron's staff was turned into a snake by God and then swallowed the snakes that came from the rods of Pharaoh's magicians.

After several turns, he sat down again. As he threw his head back in the chair, his glance happened to rest upon a bell, a disused bell, that hung in the room, and communicated for some purpose now forgotten with a chamber in the highest story of the building. [44] It was with great astonishment, and with a strange, inexplicable dread, that as he looked, he saw this bell begin to swing. It swung so softly in the outset that it scarcely made a sound; but soon it rang out loudly, and so did every bell in the house.

This might have lasted half a minute, or a minute, but it seemed an hour. The bells ceased as they had begun, together. They were succeeded by a clanking noise, deep down below; as if some person were dragging a heavy chain over the casks in the wine-merchant's cellar. Scrooge then remembered to have heard that ghosts in haunted houses were described as dragging chains.

The cellar-door flew open with a booming sound, [45] and then he heard the noise much louder, on the floors below; then coming up the stairs; then coming straight towards his door.

"It's humbug still!" said Scrooge. "I won't believe it."

His colour changed though, when, without a pause, it came on through the heavy door, and passed into the room before his eyes. Upon its coming in, the dying flame leaped up, as though it cried, "I know him! Marley's Ghost!" and fell again.

The same face: the very same. Marley in his pigtail, usual waistcoat, tights, and boots; the tassels on the latter bristling, like his pigtail, and his coat-skirts, and the hair upon his head. The chain he drew was clasped about his middle. It was long, and wound about him like a tail; and it was made (for Scrooge observed it closely) of cash-boxes, keys, padlocks,

[44] Conspicuous for its vagueness, the description of the bell that heralds Marley (as bells act as divine heralds throughout *Carol*) seems to contain another pun—one critical of Scrooge's faith. The "disused" bell (voice) used to communicate "for some purpose now forgotten" (loss of faith) with the "highest story" (the heavenly realms).

[45] Marley's ghost comes from below, the symbolic location of hell.

[46] Marley's chain gives
an account of his actions on
earth, as every man must do
before God (Romans 14:12).

[47] For thousands of years,
different parts of the body
were thought to be sources
for different emotions; the
bowels were referred to as
the seat of compassion, as
in 1 John 3:17 (*KJV*): "But
whoso hath this world's
good, and seeth his brother
have need, and shutteth up
his bowels of compassion
from him, how dwelleth
the love of God in him?" In
Carol, if Marley lacked bowels, he lacked compassion.

ledgers, deeds, and heavy purses wrought in steel. [46]
His body was transparent: so that Scrooge, observing
him, and looking through his waistcoat, could see
the two buttons on his coat behind.

Scrooge had often heard it said that Marley had
no bowels, but he had never believed it until now. [47]

No, nor did he believe it even now. Though he
looked the phantom through and through, and saw it
standing before him; though he felt the chilling influence of its death-cold eyes; and marked the very tex-
ture of the folded kerchief bound about its head and
chin, which wrapper he had not observed before: he
was still incredulous, and fought against his senses.

"How now!" said Scrooge, caustic and cold as
ever. "What do you want with me?"

"Much!"—Marley's voice, no doubt about it.

"Who are you?"

"Ask me who I *was*."

"Who *were* you then?" said Scrooge, raising his
voice. "You're particular—for a shade." He was going
to say "*to* a shade," but substituted this, as more
appropriate.

"In life I was your partner, Jacob Marley."

"Can you—can you sit down?" asked Scrooge,
looking doubtfully at him.

"I can."

"Do it then."

Scrooge asked the question, because he didn't
know whether a ghost so transparent might find
himself in a condition to take a chair; and felt that
in the event of its being impossible, it might involve
the necessity of an embarrassing explanation. But the
ghost sat down on the opposite side of the fire-place,
as if he were quite used to it.

"You don't believe in me," observed the Ghost.

"I don't," said Scrooge.

"What evidence would you have of my reality beyond that of your senses?"

"I don't know," said Scrooge.

"Why do you doubt your senses?"

"Because," said Scrooge, "a little thing affects them. A slight disorder of the stomach makes them cheats. You may be an undigested bit of beef, a blot of mustard, a crumb of cheese, a fragment of an underdone potato. There's more of gravy than of grave about you, whatever you are!"

Scrooge was not much in the habit of cracking jokes, nor did he feel, in his heart, by any means waggish [48] then. The truth is, that he tried to be smart, as a means of distracting his own attention, and keeping down his terror; for the spectre's voice disturbed the very marrow in his bones.

[48] *Waggish* means mischievous, or in a joking manner.

To sit, staring at those fixed, glazed eyes, in silence for a moment, would play, Scrooge felt, the very deuce with him. There was something very awful, too, in the spectre's being provided with an infernal atmosphere of its own. Scrooge could not feel it himself, but this was clearly the case; for though the Ghost sat perfectly motionless, its hair, and skirts, and tassels, were still agitated as by the hot vapour from an oven. [49]

[49] Dickens's use of "hot vapour from an oven" recalls the flames of hell.

"You see this toothpick?" said Scrooge, returning quickly to the charge, for the reason just assigned; and wishing, though it were only for a second, to divert the vision's stony gaze from himself.

"I do," replied the Ghost.

"You are not looking at it," said Scrooge.

"But I see it," said the Ghost, "notwithstanding."

"Well!" returned Scrooge, "I have but to swallow this, and be for the rest of my days persecuted by a legion of goblins, all of my own creation. Humbug, I tell you—humbug!"

At this the spirit raised a frightful cry, and shook

its chain with such a dismal and appalling noise, that Scrooge held on tight to his chair, to save himself from falling in a swoon. But how much greater was his horror, when the phantom taking off the bandage round its head, as if it were too warm to wear indoors, its lower jaw dropped down upon its breast!

Scrooge fell upon his knees, and clasped his hands before his face.

"Mercy!" he said. "Dreadful apparition, why do you trouble me?"

"Man of the worldly mind!" replied the Ghost, "do you believe in me or not?"

"I do," said Scrooge. "I must. But why do spirits walk the earth, and why do they come to me?"

"It is required of every man," the Ghost returned, "that the spirit within him should walk abroad among his fellow-men, and travel far and wide; [50] and if that spirit goes not forth in life, it is condemned to do so after death. It is doomed to wander through the world—oh, woe is me!—and witness what it cannot share, but might have shared on earth, and turned to happiness!"

Again the spectre raised a cry, and shook its chain, and wrung its shadowy hands.

"You are fettered," said Scrooge, trembling. "Tell me why?"

"I wear the chain I forged in life," replied the Ghost. "I made it link by link, and yard by yard; I girded it on of my own free will, and of my own free will I wore it. Is its pattern strange to *you*?"

Scrooge trembled more and more.

"Or would you know," pursued the Ghost, "the weight and length of the strong coil you bear yourself? It was full as heavy and as long as this, seven Christmas Eves ago. You have laboured on it, since. It is a ponderous chain!"

[50] What Marley describes is very close to the Great Commission of Mark 16:15, 16 "Go into all the world and preach the good news to all creation. Whoever believes and is baptized will be saved, but whoever does not believe will be condemned."

Scrooge glanced about him on the floor, in the expectation of finding himself surrounded by some fifty or sixty fathoms of iron cable: but he could see nothing.

"Jacob," he said, imploringly. "Old Jacob Marley, tell me more. Speak comfort to me, Jacob!"

"I have none to give," the Ghost replied. "It comes from other regions, Ebenezer Scrooge, and is conveyed by other ministers, [51] to other kinds of men. Nor can I tell you what I would. A very little more, is all permitted to me. I cannot rest, I cannot stay, I cannot linger anywhere. [52] My spirit never walked beyond our counting-house—mark me!—in life my spirit never roved beyond the narrow limits of our money-changing hole; and weary journeys lie before me!"

It was a habit with Scrooge, whenever he became thoughtful, to put his hands in his breeches pockets. Pondering on what the Ghost had said, he did so now, but without lifting up his eyes, or getting off his knees.

"You must have been very slow about it, Jacob," Scrooge observed, in a business-like manner, though with humility and deference.

"Slow!" the Ghost repeated.

"Seven years dead," mused Scrooge. "And travelling all the time!"

"The whole time," said the Ghost. "No rest, no peace. Incessant torture of remorse."

"You travel fast?" said Scrooge.

"On the wings of the wind," replied the Ghost.

"You might have got over a great quantity of ground in seven years," said Scrooge.

The Ghost, on hearing this, set up another cry, and clanked its chain so hideously in the dead silence of the night, that the Ward would have been justified in indicting it for a nuisance.

[51] By "other regions," Marley means heaven, and by "other ministers," he means the heavenly host. Marley speaks in veiled language because, according to a Christian tradition that Dickens follows here, Christ is not known and cannot be named in hell.

[52] From earlier drafts, Dickens changed these lines from "I may not rest, I may not stay, I may not linger anywhere," to "I cannot rest, I cannot stay, I cannot linger anywhere" to clarify that the spirit, unlike the living, has no choice but is directed by a higher power.

[53] In public readings, to drive home his meaning, Dickens changed "captive, bound, and double-ironed" to "blind man, blind man."

[54] Just as Dickens believed in the good news of the "Carol Philosophy," he also believed in the bad news (which reinforces the good news), as he wrote about in *The Life of Our Lord*, his retelling of the gospel for his children: "those who are too busy with their own profits and pleasures to think of God and of doing good, will not find such favour with Him as the sick and miserable [who do as God wants]."

[55] In public readings, Dickens altered "Yet such was I! Oh! such was I!" to the more complete—not to mention more critical and more cautionary—"I was like this man! I once was like this man!"

[56] In these few lines, Dickens summarizes the core of Christian teaching.

[57] Despite his veiled language, Marley makes his sin plain: he failed to follow Christ, and more specifically, he failed to follow Christ's example by serving the poor.

"Oh! captive, bound, and double-ironed," [53] cried the phantom, "not to know, that ages of incessant labour by immortal creatures, for this earth must pass into eternity before the good of which it is susceptible is all developed. Not to know that any Christian spirit working kindly in its little sphere, whatever it may be, will find its mortal life too short for its vast means of usefulness. Not to know that no space of regret can make amends for one life's opportunities misused! [54] Yet such was I! Oh! such was I!" [55]

"But you were always a good man of business, Jacob," faultered Scrooge, who now began to apply this to himself.

"Business!" cried the Ghost, wringing its hands again. "Mankind was my business. The common welfare was my business; charity, mercy, forbearance, and benevolence, were, all, my business. The dealings of my trade were but a drop of water in the comprehensive ocean of my business!" [56]

It held up its chain at arm's length, as if that were the cause of all its unavailing grief, and flung it heavily upon the ground again.

"At this time of the rolling year," the spectre said, "I suffer most. Why did I walk through crowds of fellow-beings with my eyes turned down, and never raise them to that blessed Star which led the Wise Men to a poor abode! [57] Were there no poor homes to which its light would have conducted *me!*"

Scrooge was very much dismayed to hear the spectre going on at this rate, and began to quake exceedingly.

"Hear me!" cried the Ghost. "My time is nearly gone."

"I will," said Scrooge. "But don't be hard upon me! Don't be flowery, Jacob! Pray!"

"How it is that I appear before you in a shape that

you can see, I may not tell. I have sat invisible beside you many and many a day."

It was not an agreeable idea. Scrooge shivered, and wiped the perspiration from his brow.

"That is no light part of my penance," pursued the Ghost. "I am here to-night to warn you, that you have yet a chance and hope of escaping my fate. A chance and hope of my procuring, Ebenezer."

"You were always a good friend to me," said Scrooge. "Thank'ee!"

"You will be haunted," resumed the Ghost, "by Three Spirits."

Scrooge's countenance fell almost as low as the Ghost's had done.

"Is that the chance and hope you mentioned, Jacob?" he demanded, in a faultering voice.

"It is."

"I—I think I'd rather not," said Scrooge.

"Without their visits," said the Ghost, "you cannot hope to shun the path I tread. Expect the first to-morrow, when the bell [58] tolls one."

[58] Church bell, to be exact.

"Couldn't I take 'em all at once, and have it over, Jacob?" hinted Scrooge.

"Expect the second on the next night at the same hour. The third upon the next night when the last stroke of twelve has ceased to vibrate. [59] Look to see me no more; and look that, for your own sake, you remember what has passed between us!"

When it had said these words, the spectre took its wrapper from the table, and bound it round its head, as before. Scrooge knew this, by the smart sound its teeth made, when the jaws were brought together by the bandage. He ventured to raise his eyes again, and found his supernatural visitor confronting him in an erect attitude, with its chain wound over and about its arm.

[59] Dickens sets Scrooge's journey over three days— three being a biblically significant number, representing not only the Holy Trinity, but the three days of Christ's death, burial, and resurrection, which Scrooge's experience echoes. In addition, the miser's journey ends on a holy day, Christmas, the day that marks the birth of Christ—and the rebirth of Scrooge.

The apparition walked backward from him; and at every step it took, the window raised itself a little, so that when the spectre reached it, it was wide open. It beckoned Scrooge to approach, which he did. When they were within two paces of each other, Marley's Ghost held up its hand, warning him to come no nearer. Scrooge stopped.

Not so much in obedience, as in surprise and fear: for on the raising of the hand, he became sensible of confused noises in the air; incoherent sounds of lamentation and regret; wailings inexpressibly sorrowful and self-accusatory. The spectre, after listening for a moment, joined in the mournful dirge; and floated out upon the bleak, dark night.

Scrooge followed to the window: desperate in his curiosity. He looked out.

The air was filled with phantoms, wandering hither and thither in restless haste, and moaning as they went. Every one of them wore chains [60] like Marley's Ghost; some few (they might be guilty governments) were linked together; none were free. Many had been personally known to Scrooge in their lives. He had been quite familiar with one old ghost, in a white waistcoat, with a monstrous iron safe attached to its ankle, who cried piteously at being unable to assist a wretched woman with an infant, whom it saw below, upon a door-step. The misery with them all was, clearly, that they sought to interfere, for good, in human matters, and had lost the power for ever.

Whether these creatures faded into mist, or mist enshrouded them, he could not tell. But they and their spirit voices faded together; and the night became as it had been when he walked home.

Scrooge closed the window, and examined the door by which the Ghost had entered. It was double-

[60] This image of spirits as prisoners calls to mind 1 Peter 3:19, when Peter spoke of the time when Christ "went and preached unto the spirits in prison."

locked, as he had locked it with his own hands, and the bolts were undisturbed. He tried to say "Humbug!" but stopped at the first syllable. And being, from the emotion he had undergone, or the fatigues of the day, or his glimpse of the Invisible World, or the dull conversation of the Ghost, or the lateness of the hour, much in need of repose; went straight to bed, without undressing, and fell asleep upon the instant.

Selfishness

About these studies: The discussion material has been designed for use with readers across a range of ages. Though all of the questions are suitable for use with adults, we would suggest that the A. and B. questions would be more appropriate for younger readers.

I. TELLING THE STORY

Stave One introduces Ebenezer Scrooge—a man so self-centered, not even Christmastime can put him in a giving mood. In this discussion we'll examine how selfishness is really our attempt to control our own lives, rather than allow God to lead us. We'll see how selfishness can cut us off from others, putting us in prisons of our own making. We'll also witness the freedom that selflessness can bring. And we'll discover what Jacob Marley laments: that selfishness can not only cheat people out of enjoying an abundant life on earth, but it can also rob them of the greatest treasure anyone could ever have—eternal life with God.

Key Verse

"Do nothing out of selfish ambition or vain conceit, but in humility consider others better than yourselves."
—PHILIPPIANS 2:3

A. How did Scrooge show his selfishness in the way he acted toward his clerk? toward his nephew? toward the two gentlemen?

B. When his nephew wished Scrooge "A merry Christmas!" Ebenezer replied with "Bah! Humbug!" In other words, he was calling Christmas a bunch of nonsense. Considering what was said in the story, why does Scrooge think Christmas is nonsense? For what other reasons would you think Scrooge might not want to celebrate the birth of Christ?

C. What connections do you see between Scrooge's material, emotional, and spiritual selfishness? How do you see each of these impacting Scrooge's life in Stave One?

D. Jacob Marley tells Scrooge that "no space of regret can make amends for one life's opportunities misused." What opportunities did Marley misuse? What opportunities do we see Scrooge misuse due to his selfishness?

II. TELLING YOUR STORY

If it wasn't for acting selfish, some of us wouldn't know how to act. Like little Scrooges, selfish people seem to think, "If I don't get it for myself, how else will I get what I want before someone else gets it?" However, we should think about what we are giving away while we are trying so hard to grab things. Instead of filling our lives up with stuff, we should be willing to give our very lives for the sake of Christ. In an amazing way, when we give our lives to God, and let go of our control, we gain more satisfaction and security than we could ever imagine.

Key Verse
"What good is it for a man to gain the whole world,
yet forfeit his soul?"
—MARK 8:36

A. Describe a time when you were selfish. What happened? How did you feel about yourself at the time?

We often think of *generosity* just meaning being willing to give money or things away. But the word *generous* also can be used to talk about someone being kind even when he or she is being treated unkindly. We see examples of generous spirits in the characters of the clerk (Bob Cratchit) and Scrooge's nephew. Describe a time when you were generous. How did people react to your generosity? What effect did being generous have on you?

C. Have you or has anyone you know ever suffered because of someone else's selfishness? How was that handled? What have you sacrificed for your own selfishness?

D. Compare the actions and attitudes of Scrooge's nephew and his clerk with those of Scrooge himself. For example, look at the two paragraphs that describe the clerk and Scrooge leaving after the day of work is done. How were the nephew and the clerk richer than the old miser? How were they more free?

III. Telling the Story of Christmas

"The people walking in darkness have seen a great light; on those living in the land of the shadow of death a light has dawned. . . . For to us a child is born, to us a son is given" (Isaiah 9:2, 6). God completed the ultimate act of selflessness by giving us his Son to bring light to our dark world, to save us from our sins. To celebrate and show our gratitude for this gift, we should act in love toward others just as God has acted in love toward us.

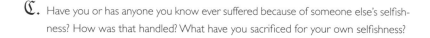

Key Verse

"Be kind and compassionate to one another, forgiving each other, just as in Christ God forgave you."
—Ephesians 4:32

A. What's the best gift you have ever received for Christmas? What made it special?

B. How can you share the gift of Christ? Why is it important to do this?

C. Scrooge was given the gift of the appearance of Marley on Christmas Eve. Marley said he had come to warn Scrooge, that he might have "a chance and hope" of escaping Marley's fate. Why do you think a character such as Marley would have wanted to give Scrooge this chance?

D. If your selfishness has separated you from others in your life, what can you do to repair these broken bonds? What practical things can you do to show others what Christmas means to you?

IV. LIVING THE STORY

Selfishness can destroy relationships: with your family, with your friends, with your God. Acting in humility and generosity can build relationships. In being humble, you seek to meet the needs of others before your own. In being generous, you seek to give more than you get.

Ask God to help you live with less selfishness and more generosity by:
✦ Showing love to someone—even when you don't feel like it.
✦ Giving of your money or time—even when it is not convenient.
✦ Praying for someone—even when they have mistreated you.

For Further Study

Psalm 119:36
Proverbs 11:17; 18:1
Luke 12:15, 20, 21
Romans 2:7, 8
Ephesians 5:5, 21
James 3:13-17

The First of the Three Spirits

[1] The third church Dickens references is thought to be St. Andrew Undershaft, according to Gwen Major, in "Scrooge's Chambers." This church was named as such due to the large shaft of a maypole that was erected near it for annual May Day celebrations.

[2] A *repeater* is a kind of watch or clock with a striking device in it that can allow it to indicate the hour or quarter hour.

[3] Dickens evokes another image from the Bible. Aside from a solar eclipse, which Scrooge does not guess at, for the sun to be blotted out would be an event of biblical proportions, as at the death of Christ (Luke 23:44, 45)—appropriate, for at the start, Scrooge is dead to Christ.

When Scrooge awoke, it was so dark, that looking out of bed, he could scarcely distinguish the transparent window from the opaque walls of his chamber. He was endeavouring to pierce the darkness with his ferret eyes, when the chimes of a neighbouring church [1] struck the four quarters. So he listened for the hour.

To his great astonishment the heavy bell went on from six to seven, and from seven to eight, and regularly up to twelve; then stopped. Twelve! It was past two when he went to bed. The clock was wrong. An icicle must have got into the works. Twelve!

He touched the spring of his repeater, [2] to correct this most preposterous clock. Its rapid little pulse beat twelve; and stopped.

"Why, it isn't possible," said Scrooge, "that I can have slept through a whole day and far into another night. It isn't possible that anything has happened to the sun, [3] and this is twelve at noon!"

The idea being an alarming one, he scrambled out of bed, and groped his way to the window. He was obliged to rub the frost off with the sleeve of his dressing-gown before he could see anything; and could see very little then. All he could make out was, that it was still very foggy and extremely cold, and that there was no noise of people running to and fro, and making a great stir, as there unquestionably would have been if night had beaten off bright day, and taken possession of the world. This was a great relief, because "three days after sight of this First of Exchange pay to Mr. Ebenezer Scrooge or his order," and so forth, would have become a mere United States' security if there were no days to count by. [4]

Scrooge went to bed again, and thought, and thought, and thought it over and over and over, and could make nothing of it. The more he thought, the more perplexed he was; and the more he endeavoured not to think, the more he thought. Marley's Ghost bothered him exceedingly. Every time he resolved within himself, after mature inquiry, that it was all a dream, his mind flew back again, like a strong spring released, to its first position, and presented the same problem to be worked all through, "Was it a dream or not?"

Scrooge lay in this state until the chimes had gone three quarters more, when he remembered, on a sudden, that the Ghost had warned him of a visitation when the bell tolled one. He resolved to lie awake until the hour was past; and, considering that he could no more go to sleep than go to Heaven, [5] this was perhaps the wisest resolution in his power.

The quarter was so long, that he was more than once convinced he must have sunk into a doze unconsciously, and missed the clock. At length it broke upon his listening ear.

"Ding, dong!"

"A quarter past," said Scrooge, counting.

"Ding, dong!"

[4] Scrooge is so focused on money that, were the sun blotted out, his biggest concern is that the people who owe him money will not be able to count the days to pay him in a timely manner and his accounts would not be settled appropriately. The reference to the "mere United States' security" actually means no security. At the time, many individual states had borrowed from English funders, and then refused to pay back the debt due to the Panic of 1837.

[5] This line carries a dual meaning: 1) Scrooge cannot physically go to heaven now, just as he cannot physically go to sleep; and 2) Scrooge cannot spiritually go to heaven now, because of the current state of his heart.

[6] Light accompanies both this Spirit and the second Spirit (but the third Spirit will be shrouded in darkness). In biblical symbolism, light represents righteousness and by extension salvation, as when Jesus uses "light of the world" to refer to both his followers (Matthew 5:14) and himself (John 8:12).

[7] The childlike appearance of this Spirit suggests the German character of the Christ Child, the Christkind. Some legends say this was a heavenly messenger said to have announced the birth of Christ, some say it is Christ as a child himself, some say the character comes from a story about a child who brought the baby Jesus gifts. But in parts of Germany and some other countries, it is the Christkind, often depicted in a white gown with a wreath of candles on its head, who brings children their gifts—not Santa Claus.

[8] This Spirit, being at once old, young, and a spirit, reflects elements of the Holy Trinity—Father, Son, and Holy Spirit.

"Half-past!" said Scrooge.

"Ding, dong!"

"A quarter to it," said Scrooge.

"Ding, dong!"

"The hour itself," said Scrooge, triumphantly, "and nothing else!"

He spoke before the hour bell sounded, which it now did with a deep, dull, hollow, melancholy One. Light [6] flashed up in the room upon the instant, and the curtains of his bed were drawn.

The curtains of his bed were drawn aside, I tell you, by a hand. Not the curtains at his feet, nor the curtains at his back, but those to which his face was addressed. The curtains of his bed were drawn aside; and Scrooge, starting up into a half-recumbent attitude, found himself face to face with the unearthly visitor who drew them: as close to it as I am now to you, and I am standing in the spirit at your elbow.

It was a strange figure—like a child: [7] yet not so like a child as like an old man, [8] viewed through some supernatural medium, which gave him the appearance of having receded from the view, and being diminished to a child's proportions. Its hair, which hung about its neck and down its back, was white as if with age; and yet the face had not a wrinkle in it, and the tenderest bloom was on the skin. The arms were very long and muscular; the hands the same, as if its hold were of uncommon strength. Its legs and feet, most delicately formed, were, like those upper members, bare. It wore a tunic of the purest white; and round its waist was bound a lustrous belt, the sheen of which was beautiful. It held a branch of fresh green holly in its hand; and, in singular contradiction of that wintry emblem, had its dress trimmed with summer flowers. But the strangest thing about it was, that from the crown of its head there sprung a bright clear jet of light, by which all this was visible; and which was doubtless the occasion of its using, in its duller moments, a great extinguisher for a cap, which it now held under its arm. [9]

Even this, though, when Scrooge looked at it with increasing steadiness, was *not* its strangest quality. For as its belt sparkled and glittered now in one part and now in another, and what was light one instant, at another time was dark, so the figure itself fluctuated in its distinctness: being now a thing with one arm, now with one leg, now with twenty legs, now a pair of legs without a head, now a head without a body: of which dissolving parts, no outline would be visible in the dense gloom wherein they melted away. And in the very wonder of this, it would be itself again; distinct and clear as ever.

"Are you the Spirit, sir, whose coming was foretold to me?" asked Scrooge.

"I am!"

The voice was soft and gentle. Singularly low, as if instead of being so close beside him, it were at a distance.

"Who, and what are you?" Scrooge demanded.

"I am the Ghost of Christmas Past."

"Long past?" inquired Scrooge: observant of its dwarfish stature.

"No. Your past."

Perhaps, Scrooge could not have told anybody why, if anybody could have asked him; but he had a special desire to see the Spirit in his cap; and begged him to be covered.

"What!" exclaimed the Ghost, "would you so soon put out, with worldly hands, the light I give? Is it not enough that you are one of those whose passions [10] made this cap, and force me through whole trains of years to wear it low upon my brow!"

[9] Some Christian readers interpret Scrooge's visitations as a dream—Scrooge himself suggests that explanation just before the first Spirit appears. Here, the light on the Spirit's head and the extinguisher cap in his arms seem to indicate that Scrooge is actually gazing dreamily at his bedside candle and extinguisher.

[10] Dickens uses *passions* as a euphemism for sins. Those who do not wish to remember their sinful past have "put out, with worldly hands, the light" the Spirit gives.

Scrooge reverently disclaimed all intention to offend, or any knowledge of having wilfully "bonneted" the Spirit at any period of his life. He then made bold to inquire what business brought him there.

"Your welfare!" said the Ghost.

Scrooge expressed himself much obliged, but could not help thinking that a night of unbroken rest would have been more conducive to that end. The Spirit must have heard him thinking, for it said immediately:

"Your reclamation, [11] then. Take heed!"

It put out its strong hand as it spoke, and clasped him gently by the arm.

"Rise! and walk with me!"

It would have been in vain for Scrooge to plead that the weather and the hour were not adapted to pedestrian purposes; that bed was warm, and the thermometer a long way below freezing; that he was clad but lightly in his slippers, dressing-gown, and nightcap; and that he had a cold upon him at that time. [12] The grasp, though gentle as a woman's hand, was not to be resisted. He rose: but finding that the Spirit made towards the window, clasped his robe in supplication.

"I am a mortal," Scrooge remonstrated, "and liable to fall."

"Bear but a touch of my hand *there*," said the Spirit, laying it upon his heart, "and you shall be upheld in more than this!" [13]

As the words were spoken, they passed through the wall, and stood upon an open country road, with fields on either hand. The city had entirely vanished. Not a vestige of it was to be seen. The darkness and the mist had vanished with it, for it was a clear, cold, winter day, with snow upon the ground.

[11] When the Spirit says he is there for Scrooge's "welfare," the worldly-minded miser thinks of his physical well-being, causing the Spirit to clarify with "reclamation," or spiritual rehabilitation.

[12] Dickens seems to satirize our list of excuses for not following the Spirit, so to speak.

[13] Another exchange of fleshly thinking versus spiritual understanding: while Scrooge says he is "liable to fall" in the physical sense, the Spirit takes it in the moral sense and entreats Scrooge to open his heart to him—"and you shall be upheld in more than this!"

"Good Heaven!" [14] said Scrooge, clasping his hands together, as he looked about him. "I was bred in this place. I was a boy here!"

The Spirit gazed upon him mildly. Its gentle touch, though it had been light and instantaneous, appeared still present to the old man's sense of feeling. He was conscious of a thousand odours floating in the air, each one connected with a thousand thoughts, and hopes, and joys, and cares long, long, forgotten!

"Your lip is trembling," said the Ghost. "And what is that upon your cheek?"

Scrooge muttered, with an unusual catching in his voice, that it was a pimple; [15] and begged the Ghost to lead him where he would.

"You recollect the way?" inquired the Spirit.

"Remember it!" cried Scrooge with fervour—"I could walk it blindfold."

"Strange to have forgotten it for so many years!" [16] observed the Ghost. "Let us go on."

They walked along the road; Scrooge recognising every gate, and post, and tree; until a little market-town appeared in the distance, with its bridge, its church, and winding river. Some shaggy ponies now were seen trotting towards them with boys upon their backs, who called to other boys in country gigs and carts, driven by farmers. All these boys were in great spirits, and shouted to each other, until the broad fields were so full of merry music, that the crisp air laughed to hear it.

"These are but shadows of the things that have been," said the Ghost. "They have no consciousness of us."

The jocund travellers came on; and as they came, Scrooge knew and named them every one. Why was he rejoiced beyond all bounds to see them! Why did his cold eye glisten, and his heart leap up as they went past! Why was he filled with gladness when he heard them give each other Merry Christmas, as they parted at cross-roads and bye-ways, for their several homes! What was merry Christmas to Scrooge? Out upon merry Christmas! What good had it ever done to him?

"The school is not quite deserted," said the Ghost. "A solitary child, neglected by his friends, is left there still." [17]

Scrooge said he knew it. And he sobbed.

They left the high-road, by a well remembered lane, and soon approached a mansion of dull red brick, with a little weathercock-surmounted cupola, on the roof, and a bell hanging in it. It was a large house, but one of broken fortunes; for the spacious offices were little used, their walls were damp and mossy, their windows broken, and their gates decayed. Fowls clucked and strutted in the stables; and the coach-houses and sheds were over-run with grass. Nor was it more retentive of its ancient state, within; for entering the dreary hall, and glancing through the open doors of many rooms, they found them poorly furnished, cold, and vast. There was an earthy savour in the air, a chilly bareness in the place, which associated itself somehow with too much getting up by candle-light, and not too much to eat.

They went, the Ghost and Scrooge, across the hall, to a door at the back of the house. It opened before them, and disclosed a long, bare, melancholy room, made barer still by lines of plain deal forms and desks. At one of these a lonely boy was reading [18] near a feeble fire; and Scrooge sat down upon a form, and wept to see his poor forgotten self as he used to be.

Not a latent echo in the house, not a squeak and

[17] Scrooge is that "solitary child, neglected by his friends" who is "left there still"—in both the past and the present—an indictment on how our unkindness can poison the lives of others, through them infecting still more, as it had throughout the life of Scrooge.

[18] This lonely boy, while being Scrooge in the story, was also the young Charles Dickens, who, being sickly as a child, was unable to play with the other boys and so spent his time reading alone.

scuffle from the mice behind the panneling, not a drip from the half-thawed water-spout in the dull yard behind, not a sigh among the leafless boughs of one despondent poplar, not the idle swinging of an empty store-house door, no, not a clicking in the fire, but fell upon the heart of Scrooge with softening influence, and gave a freer passage to his tears.

The Spirit touched him on the arm, and pointed to his younger self, intent upon his reading. [19] Suddenly a man, in foreign garments: wonderfully real and distinct to look at: stood outside the window, with an axe stuck in his belt, and leading an ass laden with wood by the bridle.

"Why, it's Ali Baba!" [20] Scrooge exclaimed in ecstacy. "It's dear old honest Ali Baba! Yes, yes, I know! One Christmas time, when yonder solitary child was left here all alone, he *did* come, for the first time, just like that. Poor boy! And Valentine," said Scrooge, "and his wild brother, Orson; there they go! And what's his name, who was put down in his drawers, asleep, at the Gate of Damascus; don't you see him! And the Sultan's Groom turned upside-down by the Genii; there he is upon his head! Serve him right. I'm glad of it. What business had *he* to be married to the Princess!"

To hear Scrooge expending all the earnestness of his nature on such subjects, in a most extraordinary voice between laughing and crying; and to see his heightened and excited face; would have been a surprise to his business friends in the city, indeed.

"There's the Parrot!" cried Scrooge. "Green body and yellow tail, with a thing like a lettuce growing out of the top of his head; there he is! Poor Robin Crusoe, he called him, when he came home again after sailing round the island. 'Poor Robin Crusoe, where have you been, Robin Crusoe?' The man thought he was dream-

[19] As a young boy, Dickens loved a small collection of books that belonged to his father. Regretfully, the family fell into debt and Dickens had to pawn away these precious items. The characters that are mentioned in the following paragraphs come from some of his favorite stories.

[20] After the New Testament and Shakespeare's works, the book Dickens most often alludes to in his writings is *The Arabian Nights*, which includes the tale of "Ali Baba and the Forty Thieves."

ing, but he wasn't. It was the Parrot, you know. There goes Friday, running for his life to the little creek! Halloa! Hoop! Halloo!"

Then, with a rapidity of transition very foreign to his usual character, he said, in pity for his former self, "Poor boy!" and cried again.

"I wish," Scrooge muttered, putting his hand in his pocket, and looking about him, after drying his eyes with his cuff: "but it's too late now."

"What is the matter?" asked the Spirit.

"Nothing," said Scrooge. "Nothing. There was a boy singing a Christmas Carol at my door last night. I should like to have given him something: that's all." [21]

The Ghost smiled thoughtfully, and waved its hand: saying as it did so, "Let us see another Christmas!"

Scrooge's former self grew larger at the words, and the room became a little darker and more dirty. The panels shrunk, the windows cracked; fragments of plaster fell out of the ceiling, and the naked laths were shown instead; but how all this was brought about, Scrooge knew no more than you do. He only knew that it was quite correct; that everything had happened so; that there he was, alone again, when all the other boys had gone home for the jolly holidays.

He was not reading now, but walking up and down despairingly. Scrooge looked at the Ghost, and with a mournful shaking of his head, glanced anxiously towards the door.

It opened; and a little girl, much younger than the boy, came darting in, and putting her arms about his neck, and often kissing him, addressed him as her "Dear, dear brother."

"I have come to bring you home, dear brother!" said the child, clapping her tiny hands, and bending down to laugh. "To bring you home, home, home!"

[21] Scrooge feels the first pang of regret for his selfishness. We must regret before we can experience repentance.

"Home, little Fan?" [22] returned the boy.

"Yes!" said the child, brimful of glee. "Home, for good and all. Home, for ever and ever. Father is so much kinder than he used to be, that home's like Heaven! [23] He spoke so gently to me one dear night when I was going to bed, that I was not afraid to ask him once more if you might come home; and he said Yes, you should; and sent me in a coach to bring you. And you're to be a man!" said the child, opening her eyes, "and are never to come back here; but first, we're to be together all the Christmas long, and have the merriest time in all the world."

"You are quite a woman, little Fan!" exclaimed the boy.

She clapped her hands and laughed, and tried to touch his head; but being too little, laughed again, and stood on tiptoe to embrace him. Then she began to drag him, in her childish eagerness, towards the door; and he, nothing loth to go, accompanied her.

A terrible voice in the hall cried, "Bring down Master Scrooge's box, there!" and in the hall appeared the schoolmaster [24] himself, who glared on Master Scrooge with a ferocious condescension, and threw him into a dreadful state of mind by shaking hands with him. [25] He then conveyed him and his sister into the veriest old well of a shivering best-parlour that ever was seen, where the maps upon the wall, and the celestial and terrestrial globes in the windows, were waxy with cold. Here he produced a decanter of curiously light wine, and a block of curiously heavy cake, and administered instalments of those dainties to the young people: at the same time, sending out a meagre servant to offer a glass of "something" to the postboy, who answered that he thanked the gentleman, but if it was the same tap as he had tasted before, he had rather not. Master Scrooge's trunk being by this time

[22] Dickens's beloved older sister was called Fanny. Like Scrooge's sister (as will be suggested in Stave Three), Frances Dickens (1810-1848), was a talented musician; and as in Scrooge's family also, the daughter received better treatment than the son from their parents.

[23] If heaven is like their home, it is little wonder that Scrooge left the faith; after all, they almost didn't let him come home for Christmas—a small reminder for those who claim to maintain Christian homes to be always mindful of how they treat the ones who live there and leave there.

[24] This terrible schoolmaster, like unqualified educators in Dickens's other works, was the author's criticism of the poor state of education in England. Dickens, ever the defender of the defenseless, said most of these unfit teachers were in the business of trading on the helplessness of children.

[25] When Dickens's father was asked about his famous son's education, he proudly stated that his son educated himself. Though this was not entirely by choice (the family debt requiring the young Dickens to work), Dickens would have had good reason of his own to avoid schools—at Wellington House Academy in London, one of only two schools he attended, he suffered at the hand of one such terrible schoolmaster as those he would later write about.

[26] A *chaise* here is a light, horse-drawn carriage, most likely pulled by only one horse.

[27] Scrooge is uneasy because, while he loved his sister, he has not loved his nephew (nor his neighbor) as well as he should have.

[28] A *Welch wig* (or Welsh wig) was a woolen cap, thought to have been made with loose ends left outside the cap, which would give it a kind of "hairy" appearance and thus, may have been the reason for it being called a wig—suitable attire for a man called Fezziwig.

tied on to the top of the chaise, [26] the children bade the schoolmaster good-bye right willingly; and getting into it, drove gaily down the garden-sweep: the quick wheels dashing the hoar-frost and snow from off the dark leaves of the evergreens like spray.

"Always a delicate creature, whom a breath might have withered," said the Ghost. "But she had a large heart!"

"So she had," cried Scrooge. "You're right. I will not gainsay it, Spirit. God forbid!"

"She died a woman," said the Ghost, "and had, as I think, children."

"One child," Scrooge returned.

"True," said the Ghost. "Your nephew!"

Scrooge seemed uneasy in his mind; and answered briefly, "Yes." [27]

Although they had but that moment left the school behind them, they were now in the busy thoroughfares of a city, where shadowy passengers passed and repassed; where shadowy carts and coaches battled for the way, and all the strife and tumult of a real city were. It was made plain enough, by the dressing of the shops, that here too it was Christmas time again; but it was evening, and the streets were lighted up.

The Ghost stopped at a certain warehouse door, and asked Scrooge if he knew it.

"Know it!" said Scrooge. "Was I apprenticed here?"

They went in. At sight of an old gentleman in a Welch wig, [28] sitting behind such a high desk, that if he had been two inches taller he must have knocked his head against the ceiling, Scrooge cried in great excitement:

"Why, it's old Fezziwig! Bless his heart; it's Fezziwig alive again!"

Old Fezziwig laid down his pen, and looked up at the clock, which pointed to the hour of seven. [29] He rubbed his hands; adjusted his capacious waistcoat; laughed all over himself, from his shoes to his organ of benevolence; [30] and called out in a comfortable, oily, rich, fat, jovial voice:

"Yo ho, there! Ebenezer! Dick!"

Scrooge's former self, now grown a young man, came briskly in, accompanied by his fellow-'prentice.

"Dick Wilkins, to be sure!" said Scrooge to the Ghost. "Bless me, yes. There he is. He was very much attached to me, was Dick. Poor Dick! Dear, dear!"

"Yo ho, my boys!" said Fezziwig. "No more work to-night. Christmas Eve, Dick. Christmas, Ebenezer! Let's have the shutters up," cried old Fezziwig, with a sharp clap of his hands, "before a man can say, Jack Robinson!"

You wouldn't believe how those two fellows went at it! They charged into the street with the shutters—one, two, three—had 'em up in their places—four, five, six—barred 'em and pinned 'em—seven, eight, nine—and came back before you could have got to twelve, panting like race-horses.

"Hilli-ho!" cried old Fezziwig, skipping down from the high desk, with wonderful agility. "Clear away, my lads, and let's have lots of room here! Hilli-ho, Dick! Chirrup, Ebenezer!"

Clear away! There was nothing they wouldn't have cleared away, or couldn't have cleared away, with old Fezziwig looking on. [31] It was done in a minute. Every movable was packed off, as if it were dismissed from public life for evermore; the floor was swept and watered, the lamps were trimmed, fuel was heaped upon the fire; and the warehouse was as snug, and warm, and dry, and bright a ball-room, as you would desire to see upon a winter's night.

[29] The normal closing time of business was 9 PM, but Fezziwig is closing two hours early in an act of Christmas Eve charity. Compare this to how Scrooge worked his clerk to the last minute on Christmas Eve—and would've liked to work him Christmas Day!

[30] The *organ of benevolence* was a term that came from phrenology, a popular nineteenth-century pseudoscience that claimed to be able to evaluate a person's mental abilities or character from the shape of the skull. The organ of benevolence was the area just above the forehead.

[31] Note the warm respect, loyalty, and dedication that Scrooge felt toward Fezziwig—three qualities Scrooge has failed miserably to inspire in his own employee.

In came a fiddler with a music-book, and went up to the lofty desk, and made an orchestra of it, and tuned like fifty stomach-aches. In came Mrs. Fezziwig, one vast substantial smile. In came the three Miss Fezziwigs, beaming and loveable. In came the six young followers whose hearts they broke. In came all the young men and women employed in the business. In came the housemaid, with her cousin, the baker. In came the cook, with her brother's particular friend, the milkman. In came the boy from over the way, who was suspected of not having board enough from his master; trying to hide himself behind the girl from next door but one, who was proved to have had her ears pulled by her Mistress. In they all came, one after another; some shyly, some boldly, some gracefully, some awkwardly, some pushing, some pulling; in they all came, anyhow and everyhow. [32] Away they all went, twenty couple at once, hands half round and back again the other way; down the middle and up again; round and round in various stages of affectionate grouping; old top couple always turning up in the wrong place; new top couple starting off again, as soon as they got there; all top couples at last, and not a bottom one to help them. When this result was brought about, old Fezziwig, clapping his hands to stop the dance, cried out, "Well done!" and the fiddler plunged his hot face into a pot of porter, especially provided for that purpose. But scorning rest upon his reappearance, he instantly began again, though there were no dancers yet, as if the other fiddler had been carried home, exhausted, on a shutter; and he were a bran-new man resolved to beat him out of sight, or perish.

There were more dances, and there were forfeits, [33] and more dances, and there was cake, and there was negus, [34] and there was a great piece

[32] This description of the guests coming from various backgrounds and classes of society brings to mind Jesus' words of advice to his host in Luke 14. He advised him to not just invite his friends and family and wealthy neighbors to his banquets, but instead to "invite the poor, the crippled, the lame, the blind, and you will be blessed. Although they cannot repay you, you will be repaid at the resurrection of the righteous" (verses 12-14).

[33] *Forfeits* were popular Christmastime games of the time that involved players having to pay some kind of penalty for missing a turn (forfeiting). These penalties evolved from small coins to, by the early 1800s, kisses.

[34] *Negus* is a kind of mulled wine with lemon juice that was a typical seasonal drink of the time and a favorite of Dickens.

of Cold Roast, and there was a great piece of Cold Boiled, and there were mince-pies, [35] and plenty of beer. But the great effect of the evening came after the Roast and Boiled, when the fiddler (an artful dog, mind! The sort of man who knew his business better than you or I could have told it him!) struck up "Sir Roger de Coverley." Then old Fezziwig stood out to dance with Mrs. Fezziwig. Top couple too; with a good stiff piece of work cut out for them; three or four and twenty pair of partners, people who were not to be trifled with; people who *would* dance, and had no notion of walking.

But if they had been twice as many: ah, four times: old Fezziwig would have been a match for them, and so would Mrs. Fezziwig. As to *her*, she was worthy to be his partner in every sense of the term. If that's not high praise, tell me higher, and I'll use it. A positive light appeared to issue from Fezziwig's calves. They shone in every part of the dance like moons. You couldn't have predicted, at any given time, what would have become of 'em next. And when old Fezziwig and Mrs. Fezziwig had gone all through the dance; advance and retire, hold hands with your partner; bow and curtsey; corkscrew; thread-the-needle, and back again to your place; Fezziwig "cut"—cut so deftly, that he appeared to wink with his legs, and came upon his feet again without a stagger. [36]

When the clock struck eleven, this domestic ball broke up. Mr. and Mrs. Fezziwig took their stations, one on either side of the door, and shaking hands with every person individually as he or she went out, wished him or her a Merry Christmas. When everybody had retired but the two 'prentices, they did the same to them; and thus the cheerful voices died away, and the lads were left to their beds; which were under a counter in the back-shop.

[35] Mince pie, a spiced meat dish, is also called Christmas pie. Today these are usually small, round pies made of mincemeat—a mixture of finely chopped raisins, apples, spices, suet, and other ingredients. Traditionally, the pie must contain three spices (cinnamon, cloves, and nutmeg) to represent the three gifts of the Magi. In honor of Christ's birth, the pie is oblong in shape to resemble the manger. On top is a flat place shaped like a star—like the one that led the wise men to the baby Jesus—on which to set a Christ-child figurine.

[36] Several dance moves are mentioned here. This last one, the "cut," shows Fezziwig's agility as he was able to jump into the air and alternate his feet rapidly in front of each other before coming back to the ground.

During the whole of this time, Scrooge had acted like a man out of his wits. His heart and soul were in the scene, and with his former self. He corroborated everything, remembered everything, enjoyed everything, and underwent the strangest agitation. It was not until now, when the bright faces of his former self and Dick were turned from them, that he remembered the Ghost, and became conscious that it was looking full upon him, while the light upon its head burnt very clear.

"A small matter," said the Ghost, "to make these silly folks so full of gratitude."

"Small!" echoed Scrooge.

The Spirit signed to him to listen to the two apprentices, who were pouring out their hearts in praise of Fezziwig: and when he had done so, said,

"Why! Is it not? He has spent but a few pounds of your mortal money: three or four, perhaps. Is that so much that he deserves this praise?"

"It isn't that," said Scrooge, heated by the remark, and speaking unconsciously like his former, not his latter, self. "It isn't that, Spirit. He has the power to render us happy or unhappy; to make our service light or burdensome; a pleasure or a toil. [37] Say that his power lies in words and looks; in things so slight and insignificant that it is impossible to add and count 'em up: what then? The happiness he gives, is quite as great as if it cost a fortune."

He felt the Spirit's glance, and stopped.

"What is the matter?" asked the Ghost.

"Nothing particular," said Scrooge.

"Something, I think?" the Ghost insisted.

"No," said Scrooge, "No. I should like to be able to say a word or two to my clerk just now! That's all." [38]

His former self turned down the lamps as he gave utterance to the wish; and Scrooge and the Ghost again stood side by side in the open air.

[37] These attributes of kind Fezziwig, which Scrooge sees should also apply to himself, are an earthly reflection of the kindness of Christ, as in Matthew 11:28 (KJV): "Come unto me, all ye that labour and are heavy laden, and I will give you rest."

[38] Scrooge feels the second pang of regret for his selfishness. Before his time with this Spirit is done, he will regret his sins three times—as Dickens continues his strategic use of the biblically significant number.

"My time grows short," observed the Spirit. "Quick!"

This was not addressed to Scrooge, or to any one whom he could see, but it produced an immediate effect. For again Scrooge saw himself. He was older now; a man in the prime of life. His face had not the harsh and rigid lines of later years; but it had begun to wear the signs of care and avarice. There was an eager, greedy, restless motion in the eye, which showed the passion that had taken root, and where the shadow of the growing tree would fall. [39]

He was not alone, but sat by the side of a fair young girl in a mourning-dress: in whose eyes there were tears, which sparkled in the light that shone out of the Ghost of Christmas Past.

"It matters little," she said, softly. "To you, very little. Another idol has displaced me; and if it can cheer and comfort you in time to come, as I would have tried to do, I have no just cause to grieve."

"What Idol has displaced you?" he rejoined.

"A golden one." [40]

"This is the even-handed dealing of the world!" he said. "There is nothing on which it is so hard as poverty; and there is nothing it professes to condemn with such severity as the pursuit of wealth!" [41]

"You fear the world too much," she answered, gently. "All your other hopes have merged into the hope of being beyond the chance of its sordid reproach. I have seen your nobler aspirations fall off one by one, until the master-passion, Gain, engrosses you. Have I not?" [42]

"What then?" he retorted. "Even if I have grown so much wiser, what then? I am not changed towards you."

She shook her head.

[39] The superstition of the "evil eye" is used to show the sinfulness of greed (see Stave One, Note 11).

[40] Dickens references the biblical account of the golden calf from Exodus 32. Just as the Israelites had formed a false god of gold in the shape of a calf, the woman here criticizes Scrooge for trading his allegiance to a sacred love for a sacrilegious one.

[41] Scrooge is caught in the vicious cycle of a worldly mindset: he justifies his worldly pursuit by condemning the harshness of the world. In this, God is not god, and neither is the world—man himself is god, free to shift his judgments based on what benefits him.

[42] Paul talked about such men engrossed by Gain in 1 Timothy 6:5, 6 (KJV) when he spoke of "perverse disputings of men of corrupt minds, and destitute of the truth, supposing that gain is godliness: from such withdraw thyself." In contrast, "godliness with contentment is great gain."

"Am I?"

"Our contract is an old one. It was made when we were both poor and content to be so, until, in good season, we could improve our worldly fortune by our patient industry. You *are* changed. When it was made, you were another man."

"I was a boy," he said impatiently.

"Your own feeling tells you that you were not what you are," she returned. "I am. That which promised happiness when we were one in heart, is fraught with misery now that we are two. How often and how keenly I have thought of this, I will not say. It is enough that I *have* thought of it, and can release you."

"Have I ever sought release?"

"In words. No. Never."

"In what, then?"

"In a changed nature; in an altered spirit; in another atmosphere of life; another Hope as its great end. In everything that made my love of any worth or value in your sight. If this had never been between us," said the girl, looking mildly, but with steadiness, upon him; "tell me, would you seek me out and try to win me now? Ah, no!"

He seemed to yield to the justice of this supposition, in spite of himself. But he said, with a struggle, "You think not."

"I would gladly think otherwise if I could," she answered, "Heaven knows! When *I* have learned a Truth like this, I know how strong and irresistible it must be. But if you were free to-day, to-morrow, yesterday, can even I believe that you would choose a dowerless girl [43]—you who, in your very confidence with her, weigh everything by Gain: or, choosing her, if for a moment you were false enough to your one guiding principle to do so, do I not know that your

[43] The woman, earlier described as wearing a mourning dress, has lost her parents (either the last living one or both at the same time) and has been left penniless. Without any money, she feels she is less attractive to Scrooge—and the "old sinner," adding insult to injury, does not deny it!

repentance and regret [44] would surely follow? I do; and I release you. With a full heart, for the love of him you once were."

He was about to speak; but with her head turned from him, she resumed.

"You may—the memory of what is past half makes me hope you will—have pain in this. A very, very brief time, and you will dismiss the recollection of it, gladly, as an unprofitable dream, [45] from which it happened well that you awoke. May you be happy in the life you have chosen!"

She left him, and they parted.

"Spirit!" said Scrooge, "show me no more! Conduct me home. Why do you delight to torture me?" [46]

"One shadow more!" exclaimed the Ghost.

"No more!" cried Scrooge. "No more. I don't wish to see it. Show me no more!"

But the relentless Ghost pinioned him in both his arms, and forced him to observe what happened next.

They were in another scene and place: a room, not very large or handsome, but full of comfort. Near to the winter fire sat a beautiful young girl, so like that last that Scrooge believed it was the same, until he saw *her*, now a comely matron, sitting opposite her daughter. The noise in this room was perfectly tumultuous, for there were more children there, than Scrooge in his agitated state of mind could count; and, unlike the celebrated herd in the poem, they were not forty children conducting themselves like one, but every child was conducting itself like forty. The consequences were uproarious beyond belief; but no one seemed to care; on the contrary, the mother and daughter laughed heartily, and enjoyed it very much; and the latter, soon beginning to mingle in the sports, got pillaged by the young

[44] Like two roadside signs, Dickens names the two biblical principles—"repentance and regret"—that Scrooge must deal with at this point in his spiritual journey.

[45] An "unprofitable dream" as opposed to a profitable one—such as the one Scrooge is having now? Dickens seems to play with the interpretation of reality in the events unfolding.

[46] To mark the moment of Scrooge's third regret, before crossing it out for the final draft, Dickens originally continued with "And as he spoke he pressed his hands against his head, and stamped upon the ground."

brigands most ruthlessly. What would I not have given to be one of them! Though I never could have been so rude, no, no! I wouldn't for the wealth of all the world have crushed that braided hair, and torn it down; and for the precious little shoe, I wouldn't have plucked it off, God bless my soul! to save my life. As to measuring her waist in sport, as they did, bold young brood, I couldn't have done it; I should have expected my arm to have grown round it for a punishment, and never come straight again. And yet I should have dearly liked, I own, to have touched her lips; to have questioned her, that she might have opened them; to have looked upon the lashes of her downcast eyes, and never raised a blush; to have let loose waves of hair, an inch of which would be a keepsake beyond price: in short, I should have liked, I do confess, to have had the lightest licence of a child, and yet been man enough to know its value.

But now a knocking at the door was heard, and such a rush immediately ensued that she with laughing face and plundered dress was borne towards it the centre of a flushed and boisterous group, just in time to greet the father, who, came home attended by a man laden with Christmas toys and presents. [47] Then the shouting and the struggling, and the onslaught that was made on the defenceless porter! The scaling him with chairs for ladders, to dive into his pockets, despoil him of brown-paper parcels, hold on tight by his cravat, hug him round the neck, pommel his back, and kick his legs in irrepressible affection! The shouts of wonder and delight with which the development of every package was received! The terrible announcement that the baby had been taken in the act of putting a doll's frying-pan into his mouth, and was more than suspected of having swallowed a fictitious

[47] Dickens was just as generous—not only with his own children, but others as well. As his daughter Mamie wrote in her book *My Father As I Recall Him* (1896): "My father used to take us, every twenty-fourth day of December, to a toy shop in Holborn, where we were allowed to select our Christmas presents, and also any that we wished to give to our little companions. Although we were often an hour or more in the shop before our several tastes were satisfied, he never showed the least impatience, was always interested, and as desirous as we, that we should choose exactly what we liked best."

turkey, glued on a wooden platter! The immense relief of finding this a false alarm! The joy, and gratitude, and ecstacy! They are all indescribable alike. It is enough that by degrees the children and their emotions got out of the parlour and by one stair at a time, up to the top of the house; where they went to bed, and so subsided.

And now Scrooge looked on more attentively than ever, when the master of the house, having his daughter leaning fondly on him, sat down with her and her mother at his own fireside; and when he thought that such another creature, quite as graceful and as full of promise, might have called him father, and been a spring-time in the haggard winter of his life, his sight grew very dim indeed.

"Belle," [48] said the husband, turning to his wife with a smile, "I saw an old friend of yours this afternoon." [49]

"Who was it?"

"Guess!"

"How can I? Tut, don't I know?" she added in the same breath, laughing as he laughed. "Mr. Scrooge."

"Mr. Scrooge it was. I passed his office window; and as it was not shut up, and he had a candle inside, I could scarcely help seeing him. His partner lies upon the point of death, I hear; and there he sat alone. Quite alone in the world, I do believe."

"Spirit!" said Scrooge in a broken voice, "remove me from this place."

"I told you these were shadows of the things that have been," said the Ghost. "That they are what they are, do not blame me!"

"Remove me!" Scrooge exclaimed, "I cannot bear it!"

He turned upon the Ghost, and seeing that it looked upon him with a face, in which in some

[48] Like the bells elsewhere in *Carol*, Dickens has this "Belle" also herald a divine message, as bitter as it is, meant for Scrooge's spiritual "reclamation" (rehabilitation).

[49] Dickens had his own "Belle," of whom he wrote to his friend Forster in January, 1855, "A sense comes always crushing on me now . . . as of one happiness I have missed in life, and one friend and companion I have never made."

[50] Scrooge wrestling with the Spirit recalls the biblical account of Jacob wrestling with a spirit from Genesis 32. In both stories, a spiritual being chastises a man for past sins, the man wrestles with the spirit as he tries to secure a favor, and the spirit is overcome.

[51] Dickens indicates that, although Scrooge fights against the Spirit, he has seen the "light"—and cannot forget its lesson.

[52] For Christian readers who interpret Scrooge's visitations as a dream, this seems the second most obvious indication (see Note 9). He finds himself drowsy in his bedroom—and apparently puts out his bedside candle before falling back to sleep.

strange way there were fragments of all the faces it had shown him, wrestled with it. [50]

"Leave me! Take me back. Haunt me no longer!"

In the struggle, if that can be called a struggle in which the Ghost with no visible resistance on its own part was undisturbed by any effort of its adversary, Scrooge observed that its light was burning high and bright; and dimly connecting that with its influence over him, he seized the extinguisher-cap, and by a sudden action pressed it down upon its head.

The Spirit dropped beneath it, so that the extinguisher covered its whole form; but though Scrooge pressed it down with all his force, he could not hide the light: [51] which streamed from under it, in an unbroken flood upon the ground.

He was conscious of being exhausted, and overcome by an irresistible drowsiness; and, further, of being in his own bedroom. He gave the cap a parting squeeze, in which his hand relaxed; and had barely time to reel to bed, before he sank into a heavy sleep. [52]

Regret

I. TELLING THE STORY

Stave Two sees Scrooge regret the mistakes of his past—even as he learns that they will haunt his future. We watch as the Ghost of Christmas Past takes Scrooge back to key points in his life—times that remind him of right actions and reveal when he first chose the love of money over a life of love. In the following study, we'll examine the opportunities Scrooge had and think about the messages God sends us all through our guilt. One of those messages is that God can and does forgive us for our past sins, and he alone can release us from a life of regret.

Key Verse

"Whatever is has already been,
and what will be has been before;
and God will call the past to account."
—ECCLESIASTES 3:15

A. In this chapter we view three periods in Scrooge's life: childhood; adolescence; and young adulthood. What regrets about his present life is he faced with as he remembers each part of his past?

B. What opportunities did Scrooge have that, if he had taken them, might have led him to a different kind of life?

C. What disappointments marked the young Ebenezer's life? What temptations did he struggle with? How did these two areas shape the choices he made?

D. As the boy Scrooge grows, so does the depth of his relationships: from imaginary playmates, to friendly coworkers, to romantic companions. And as the relationships grow in intensity, so too do his regrets. Thinking about how Scrooge lives, how do you think he dealt with the pain from his past? What messages was God trying to send him through his pain?

II. TELLING YOUR STORY

All of us would like to escape the negative consequences of our wrongful actions, but regret can have a positive effect. Sincere sorrow over our past sins can spur us on to godly actions. Rather than ignoring our regrets, we need to use them to change our lives for the better.

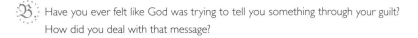

Key Verse

"The sacrifices of God are a broken spirit;
a broken and contrite heart,
O God, you will not despise."
—PSALM 51:17

A. Have you ever felt sorry for something you did? What did you do about that?

B. Have you ever felt like God was trying to tell you something through your guilt? How did you deal with that message?

C. How do you react when you are confronted by your own regrets? Do you avoid dealing with them? get angry? get depressed? try to fix the situation? How has your reaction to past guilt in your life shaped how you live in the present?

D. There are probably certain unresolved regrets that come to your mind even as we are working through this study. What do you think God wants you to understand about those situations? What steps can you take to use that regret in a positive way?

III. Telling the Story of Christmas

Regret reflects a longing to be right with God. God wants to see a broken heart, not because he wants his children to be sad, but because it reveals a person's understanding of the seriousness of their sin and its consequences for all those around. When we feel this godly sorrow, it is difficult to understand how God could ever forgive us. But that is why Jesus came—to be a living, breathing picture of God's mercy and grace. As the angel Gabriel told Mary, "Nothing is impossible with God" (Luke 1:37).

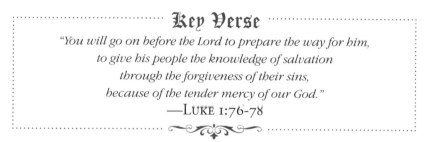

Key Verse

"You will go on before the Lord to prepare the way for him,
to give his people the knowledge of salvation
through the forgiveness of their sins,
because of the tender mercy of our God."
—LUKE 1:76-78

A. Pretend for a moment that you are one of the angels who brought a message about the coming of Jesus. What would you say to people? What would be the most important point you would want people to understand about Jesus?

B. Each person that heard the angels speak was afraid or troubled by the experience at first. What might make you afraid to listen to what God has to say to you?

C. When you come to God with your regrets, he has the power to forgive your sins and wash away your shame forever. Believing in God's power to do this is a start, but 2 Peter 1:5-9 encourages us to add to our faith the following qualities: goodness, knowledge, self-control, perseverance, godliness, brotherly kindness, and love. In fact, we're told that if we don't have these, we're "nearsighted and blind" and have forgotten that we have been cleansed from our past sins. Pick two or three of these qualities and describe how you think they can help you to keep from being "ineffective and unproductive" as you follow Christ.

𝕯. For many people, Christmas is a time of sad memories of past mistakes or losses. How can you be a living, breathing picture of God's mercy and grace to someone who may be dealing with the pain of regret?

IV. LIVING THE STORY

God wants us to regret our sinful acts, but he doesn't want us to get stuck there. Regret must be formed into action. Through listening carefully to the messages God has for us and gaining understanding about his plans, we can live lives that help to bring "Glory to God in the highest, and on earth peace to men on whom his favor rests" (Luke 2:14).

Ask God to help you change your regret into action by:

✦ Using your regret as a reminder to correct a past wrong.

✦ Using your guilt as a signal to confess sin to God.

✦ Using your understanding to change how you act in the future.

For Further Study

Proverbs 16:22; 28:16, 18

Jeremiah 2:19

John 16:5-11

Acts 24:14-16

Romans 2:12-16; 8:12-17

2 Corinthians 7:8-13

Hebrews 10:19-24

2 Peter 1:3-11

The Second of the Three Spirits

Awaking in the middle of a prodigiously tough snore, and sitting up in bed to get his thoughts together, Scrooge had no occasion to be told that the bell was again upon the stroke of One. He felt that he was restored to consciousness in the right nick of time, for the especial purpose of holding a conference [1] with the second messenger despatched to him through Jacob Marley's intervention. But finding that he turned uncomfortably cold when he began to wonder which of his curtains this new spectre would draw back, he put them every one aside with his own hands; and lying down again, established a sharp look-out all round the bed. For he wished to challenge the Spirit on the moment of its appearance, and did not wish to be taken by surprise and made nervous.

Gentlemen of the free-and-easy sort, who plume themselves on being acquainted with a move or two, and being usually equal to the time-of-day, express the wide range of their capacity for adventure by observing that they are good for anything from pitch-and-toss [2] to manslaughter; between which opposite extremes, no doubt, there lies a tolerably wide and comprehensive range of subjects. Without

[1] After the last visitation, being a bit further down the road of rehabilitation, Scrooge wants to express to the second Spirit his willingness to cooperate.

[2] *Pitch-and-toss* was a type of heads-or-tails gambling game. Dickens is talking about worldly men here, who were up for anything—even criminal activity—that might suit their purposes.

venturing for Scrooge quite as hardily as this, I don't mind calling on you to believe that he was ready for a good broad field of strange appearances, and that nothing between a baby and a rhinoceros would have astonished him very much.

Now, being prepared for almost anything, he was not by any means prepared for nothing; and, consequently, when the Bell struck One, and no shape appeared, he was taken with a violent fit of trembling. Five minutes, ten minutes, a quarter of an hour went by, yet nothing came. All this time, he lay upon his bed, the very core and centre of a blaze of ruddy light, [3] which streamed upon it when the clock proclaimed the hour; and which being only light, [4] was more alarming than a dozen ghosts, as he was powerless to make out what it meant, or would be at; and was sometimes apprehensive that he might be at that very moment an interesting case of spontaneous combustion, without having the consolation of knowing it. At last, however, he began to think—as you or I would have thought at first; for it is always the person not in the predicament who knows what ought to have been done in it, and would unquestionably have done it too—at last, I say, he began to think that the source and secret of this ghostly light might be in the adjoining room; from whence, on further tracing it, it seemed to shine. This idea taking full possession of his mind, he got up softly and shuffled in his slippers to the door.

The moment Scrooge's hand was on the lock, a strange voice called him by his name, and bade him enter. He obeyed.

It was his own room. There was no doubt about that. But it had undergone a surprising transformation. The walls and ceiling were so hung with living green, [5] that it looked a perfect grove; from every part of which,

[3] Lest we think Scrooge's willingness is all that is required for his rehabilitation, Dickens shows us much more must change by having Scrooge literally lay in the light of the second Spirit without realizing what it means.

[4] Unlike the previous Spirit which exuded clear light, the light that accompanies the second Spirit is firelight. In the Bible, fire represents divine power, as in the "tongues of fire" that rested upon the apostles at Pentecost in Acts 2:3 or the description of God as a "consuming fire" in Hebrews 12:29.

[5] Dickens uses white to color the first Spirit; green to color the second Spirit. Green is symbolically the color of growth. In *Carol*, tellingly, the rehabilitating Scrooge sees "his own room" has "undergone a surprising transformation" being covered with "living green."

bright gleaming berries glistened. The crisp leaves of holly, mistletoe, and ivy reflected back the light, as if so many little mirrors had been scattered there; and such a mighty blaze went roaring up the chimney, as that dull petrification of a hearth had never known in Scrooge's time, or Marley's, or for many and many a winter season gone. Heaped up upon the floor, to form a kind of throne, were turkeys, geese, game, poultry, brawn, great joints of meat, sucking-pigs, long wreaths of sausages, mince-pies, plum-puddings, barrels of oysters, red-hot chesnuts, cherry-cheeked apples, juicy oranges, luscious pears, immense twelfth-cakes, [6] and seething bowls of punch, that made the chamber dim with their delicious steam. In easy state upon this couch, there sat a jolly Giant, [7] glorious to see; who bore a glowing torch, in shape not unlike Plenty's horn, and held it up, high up, to shed its light on Scrooge, as he came peeping round the door.

"Come in!" exclaimed the Ghost. "Come in! and know me better, man!"

Scrooge entered timidly, and hung his head before this Spirit. He was not the dogged Scrooge he had been; and though its eyes were clear and kind, he did not like to meet them.

"I am the Ghost of Christmas Present," said the Spirit. "Look upon me!"

Scrooge reverently did so. It was clothed in one simple deep green robe, or mantle, bordered with white fur. This garment hung so loosely on the figure, that its capacious breast was bare, [8] as if disdaining to be warded or concealed by any artifice. Its feet, observable beneath the ample folds of the garment, were also bare; and on its head it wore no other covering than a holly wreath [9] set here and there with shining icicles. Its dark brown curls were long and free: free as its genial face, its sparkling eye, its open

[6] Twelfth-cakes were pastries served on Twelfth Night, the last night of celebration before Epiphany on January 6, which was held as the day the wise men reached the baby Jesus.

[7] In this Spirit, Dickens portrays the English character of Father Christmas, who is typically pictured as a "jolly Giant" in a fur-trimmed green robe and a holly crown.

[8] The breast, which contains the heart, is traditionally considered the seat of goodwill. This Spirit, as is appropriate for the season, is so overflowing with goodwill, it cannot be contained.

[9] Holly, according to a Christian tradition, symbolizes Christ: the pointed leaves suggest the crown of thorns, the red berries suggest the blood shed for our salvation and the green coloring suggests eternal life (or growth). One tradition even holds holly was used for the crown of thorns—similar to the head wreath the Spirit wears.

[10] Dickens indicates the Spirit needs no sword because he is a messenger of Christ, the Prince of Peace, who holds ultimate victory.

[11] Writing in 1843, Dickens is counting years, or Christmases, since the birth of Christ. There is a different "brother," or Spirit of Christmas Present, for each Christmas.

[12] In an earlier draft, to foreshadow the appearance of the demon children Ignorance and Want, Dickens continued: "and as it did so Scrooge observed that at its skirts it seemed to have some object which it sought to hide. He fancied that he saw either the claw of a great bird or a foot much smaller than the Spirit's own protruding for a moment from its robes; and being curious in everything concerning these unearthly visitors, he asked the Spirit what it meant.

"'They are not so many as they might be,' replied the Ghost, 'who care to know or ask. No matter what it is, just now. Are you ready to go forth with me?'"

[13] The robe of the Spirit, which aids in the spiritual healing of Scrooge when he touches it, recalls the cloak of Christ, which aids in the physical healing of a woman when she touches it, in Matthew 9:20-22.

hand, its cheery voice, its unconstrained demeanour, and its joyful air. Girded round its middle was an antique scabbard; but no sword was in it, and the ancient sheath was eaten up with rust. [10]

"You have never seen the like of me before!" exclaimed the Spirit.

"Never," Scrooge made answer to it.

"Have never walked forth with the younger members of my family; meaning (for I am very young) my elder brothers born in these later years?" pursued the Phantom.

"I don't think I have," said Scrooge. "I am afraid I have not. Have you had many brothers, Spirit?"

"More than eighteen hundred," [11] said the Ghost.

"A tremendous family to provide for!" muttered Scrooge.

The Ghost of Christmas Present rose. [12]

"Spirit," said Scrooge submissively, "conduct me where you will. I went forth last night on compulsion, and I learnt a lesson which is working now. To-night, if you have aught to teach me, let me profit by it."

"Touch my robe!" [13]

Scrooge did as he was told, and held it fast.

Holly, mistletoe, red berries, ivy, turkeys, geese, game, poultry, brawn, meat, pigs, sausages, oysters, pies, puddings, fruit, and punch, all vanished instantly. So did the room, the fire, the ruddy glow, the hour of night, and they stood in the city streets on Christmas morning, where (for the weather was severe) the people made a rough, but brisk and not unpleasant kind of music, in scraping the snow from the pavement in front of their dwellings, and from the tops of their houses: whence it was mad delight to the boys to see it come plumping down into the road below, and splitting into artificial little snow-storms.

The house fronts looked black enough, and the windows blacker, contrasting with the smooth white sheet of snow upon the roofs, and with the dirtier snow upon the ground; which last deposit had been ploughed up in deep furrows by the heavy wheels of carts and waggons; furrows that crossed and re-crossed each other hundreds of times where the great streets branched off, and made intricate channels, hard to trace in the thick yellow mud and icy water. The sky was gloomy, and the shortest streets were choked up with a dingy mist, half thawed half frozen, whose heavier particles descended in a shower of sooty atoms, as if all the chimneys in Great Britain had, by one consent, caught fire, and were blazing away to their dear hearts' content. There was nothing very cheerful in the climate or the town, and yet was there an air of cheerfulness abroad that the clearest summer air and brightest summer sun might have endeavoured to diffuse in vain.

For the people who were shovelling away on the house-tops were jovial and full of glee; calling out to one another from the parapets, and now and then exchanging a facetious snowball—better-natured missile far than many a wordy jest—laughing heartily if it went right, and not less heartily if it went wrong. The poulterers' shops were still half open, and the fruiterers' were radiant in their glory. There were great, round, pot-bellied baskets of chesnuts, shaped like the waistcoats of jolly old gentlemen, lolling at the doors, and tumbling out into the street in their apoplectic opulence. There were ruddy, brown-faced, broad-girthed Spanish Onions, shining in the fatness of their growth like Spanish Friars; and winking from their shelves in wanton slyness at the girls as they went by, and glanced demurely at the hung-up mistletoe. There were pears and apples, clustered high in blooming pyramids; there were bunches of grapes, made, in the shopkeepers' benevolence, to dangle from conspicuous hooks, that people's mouths might water gratis as they passed; there were piles of filberts, mossy and brown, recalling, in their fragrance, ancient walks among the woods, and pleasant shufflings ankle deep through withered leaves; there were Norfolk Biffins, squab and swarthy, setting off the yellow of the oranges and lemons, and, in the great compactness of their juicy persons, urgently entreating and beseeching to be carried home in paper bags and eaten after dinner. The very gold and silver fish, set forth among these choice fruits in a bowl, though members of a dull and stagnant-blooded race, appeared to know that there was something going on; and, to a fish, went gasping round and round their little world in slow and passionless excitement.

The Grocers'! oh, the Grocers'! nearly closed, with perhaps two shutters down, or one; but through those gaps such glimpses! It was not alone that the scales descending on the counter made a merry sound, or that the twine and roller parted company so briskly, or that the canisters were rattled up and down like juggling tricks, or even that the blended scents of tea and coffee were so grateful to the nose, or even that the raisins were so plentiful and rare, the almonds so extremely white, the sticks of cinnamon so long and straight, the other spices so delicious, the candied fruits so caked and spotted with molten sugar as to make the coldest lookers-on feel faint and subsequently bilious. Nor was it that the figs were moist and pulpy, or that the French plums blushed in modest tartness from their highly-decorated boxes, or that everything was good to eat and in its Christmas dress: but the customers were all so hurried and so eager in the hopeful promise of the day, that they tumbled up against each other at the door, clashing their wicker baskets wildly, and left their purchases upon the counter, and came running back to fetch them, and committed hundreds of the like mistakes in the best humour possible; while the Grocer and his people were so frank and fresh that the polished hearts with which they fastened their aprons behind might have been their own, worn outside for general inspection, and for Christmas daws to peck at if they chose.

But soon the steeples called good people all, to church and chapel, [14] and away they came, flocking through the streets in their best clothes, and with their gayest faces. And at the same time there emerged from scores of bye streets, lanes, and nameless turnings, innumerable people, carrying their dinners to the bakers' shops. The sight of these poor revellers appeared to interest the Spirit very much, for he stood with Scrooge beside him in a baker's doorway, and taking off the covers as their bearers passed, sprinkled incense [15] on their dinners from his torch. And it was a very uncommon kind of torch, for once or twice when there were angry words between some dinner-carriers who had jostled with each other, he shed a few drops of water on them from it, and their good humour was restored directly. [16] For they said, it was a shame to quarrel upon Christmas Day. And so it was! God love it, so it was!

In time the bells ceased, and the bakers' were shut up; and yet there was a genial shadowing forth of all these dinners and the progress of their cooking, in the thawed blotch of wet above each baker's oven; where the pavement smoked as if its stones were cooking too.

"Is there a peculiar flavour in what you sprinkle from your torch?" asked Scrooge.

[14] Seemingly, Dickens sets this Christmas Day on a Sunday, a holy day of the year on a holy day of the week.

[15] Originally, Dickens wrote that the Spirit sprinkled "fire," before changing it to the more contextually significant "incense"—this Spirit blesses these lowly people with the same gift as the Magi blessed the lowly Christ child.

[16] Unlike the first and third Spirits, the Present Spirit helps not only Scrooge, but others in need as well, thereby setting an example to the "present spirit" in us all.

[17] In an earlier draft, Dickens wrote, "Because my eldest brother took them especially under his protection," in reference to Jesus Christ, before altering the line to "Because it needs it most" to avoid any hint of irreverence.

[18] Scrooge is talking about so-called pious rich people of his day who wanted the bakeries closed on Sunday, which was the day of the week when poor people who had no stoves went to the bakeries to cook their dinners. They could use the ovens on Sundays because bakers were forbidden by law to bake then. Dickens objected to the inequity, writing in a pamphlet, "The Sabbath was made for man, not man to serve the Sabbath"—Christ's words in Mark 2:27.

[19] Dickens criticizes the self-righteous people noted above—through one of the very heavenly host they claim to serve.

"There is. My own."

"Would it apply to any kind of dinner on this day?" asked Scrooge.

"To any kindly given. To a poor one most."

"Why to a poor one most?" asked Scrooge.

"Because it needs it most." [17]

"Spirit," said Scrooge, after a moment's thought, "I wonder you, of all the beings in the many worlds about us, should desire to cramp these people's opportunities of innocent enjoyment."

"I!" cried the Spirit.

"You would deprive them of their means of dining every seventh day, often the only day on which they can be said to dine at all," said Scrooge. "Wouldn't you?"

"I!" cried the Spirit.

"You seek to close these places on the Seventh Day?" said Scrooge. "And it comes to the same thing."

"*I* seek!" exclaimed the Spirit.

"Forgive me if I am wrong. It has been done in your name, or at least in that of your family," [18] said Scrooge.

"There are some upon this earth of yours," returned the Spirit, "who lay claim to know us, and who do their deeds of passion, pride, ill-will, hatred, envy, bigotry, and selfishness in our name; who are as strange to us and all our kith and kin, as if they had never lived. Remember that, and charge their doings on themselves, not us." [19]

Scrooge promised that he would; and they went on, invisible, as they had been before, into the suburbs of the town. It was a remarkable quality of the Ghost (which Scrooge had observed at the baker's) that notwithstanding his gigantic size, he could accommodate himself to any place with ease; and that he stood beneath a low roof quite as gracefully and like a supernatural creature, as it was possible he could have done in any lofty hall.

And perhaps it was the pleasure the good Spirit had in showing off this power of his, or else it was his own kind, generous, hearty nature, and his sympathy with all poor men, that led him straight to Scrooge's clerk's; for there he went, and took Scrooge with him, holding to his robe; and on the threshold of the door the Spirit smiled, and stopped to bless Bob Cratchit's [20] dwelling with the sprinklings of his torch. Think of that! Bob had but fifteen "Bob" a-week himself; he pocketed on Saturdays but fifteen copies of his Christian name; [21] and yet the Ghost of Christmas Present blessed his four-roomed house! [22]

Then up rose Mrs. Cratchit, Cratchit's wife, dressed out but poorly in a twice-turned gown, but brave in ribbons, [23] which are cheap and make a goodly show for sixpence; and she laid the cloth, assisted by Belinda Cratchit, second of her daughters, also brave in ribbons; while Master Peter Cratchit plunged a fork into the saucepan of potatoes, and getting the corners of his monstrous shirt-collar (Bob's private property, conferred upon his son and heir in honour of the day) into his mouth, rejoiced to find himself so gallantly attired, and yearned to show his linen in the fashionable Parks. And now two smaller Cratchits, boy and girl, came tearing in, screaming that outside the baker's they had smelt the goose, and known it for their own; and basking in luxurious thoughts of sage-and-onion, these young Cratchits danced about the table, and exalted Master Peter Cratchit to the skies, while he (not proud, although his collars nearly choked him) blew the fire, until the slow potatoes bubbling up, knocked loudly at the saucepan-lid to be let out and peeled.

"What has ever got your precious father then,"

[20] Dickens likely got the last name "Cratchit" from the word *cratch*, which is archaic English for crèche or the manger of baby Jesus.

[21] Dickens writes in mock wonder, sarcastically censuring the view that wealth is always a sign of God's approval and poverty is always a sign of his disapproval (a "Bob" or shilling was worth only twelve pennies)—and tweaking Christians that hold this opinion by slyly evoking "Christian name" instead of given name, the more modern synonym for a first name.

[22] As a boy in London, Dickens lived with his impoverished family in such a "four-roomed house.

[23] Mrs. Cratchit's "twice-turned gown" and the attire of the whole family not only reveals their poverty, but also how much the celebration of Christmas means to them. Turning a gown involved the skilled practice of unsewing a dress completely and putting it back together with the fabric turned out to the other, less-worn, side. Mrs. Cratchit tries to hide any remaining worn places with cheap ribbons. The family put on their best duds not to impress anyone, but simply in honor of the day.

[24] The Cratchit family corresponds to the Dickens family of the four-roomed house—a poor clerk and his wife with six children, three boys and three girls.

[25] At Christmastime, low-paid London workers were at the mercy of their employers to get free for the holiday—and Martha's employer seems even less merciful than Scrooge, working her on Christmas morning!

[26] The fourth London church Dickens mentions is thought to be St. Stephan's Church.

said Mrs. Cratchit. "And your brother, Tiny Tim; and Martha [24] warn't as late last Christmas Day by half-an-hour?"

"Here's Martha, mother!" said a girl, appearing as she spoke.

"Here's Martha, mother!" cried the two young Cratchits. "Hurrah! There's *such* a goose, Martha!"

"Why, bless your heart alive, my dear, how late you are!" said Mrs. Cratchit, kissing her a dozen times, and taking off her shawl and bonnet for her, with officious zeal.

"We'd a deal of work to finish up last night," replied the girl, "and had to clear away this morning, mother!" [25]

"Well! Never mind so long as you are come," said Mrs. Cratchit. "Sit ye down before the fire, my dear, and have a warm, Lord bless ye!"

"No no! There's father coming," cried the two young Cratchits, who were everywhere at once. "Hide Martha, hide!"

So Martha hid herself, and in came little Bob, the father, with at least three feet of comforter exclusive of the fringe, hanging down before him; and his thread-bare clothes darned up and brushed, to look seasonable; and Tiny Tim upon his shoulder. Alas for Tiny Tim, he bore a little crutch, and had his limbs supported by an iron frame!

"Why, where's our Martha?" cried Bob Cratchit, looking round.

"Not coming," said Mrs. Cratchit.

"Not coming!" said Bob, with a sudden declension in his high spirits; for he had been Tim's blood horse all the way from church, [26] and had come home rampant. "Not coming upon Christmas Day!"

Martha didn't like to see him disappointed, if it were only in joke; so she came out prematurely from behind the closet door, and ran into his arms, while the two young Cratchits hustled Tiny Tim, and bore him off into the wash-house, that he might hear the pudding singing in the copper. [27]

"And how did little Tim behave?" asked Mrs. Cratchit, when she had rallied Bob on his credulity and Bob had hugged his daughter to his heart's content.

"As good as gold," said Bob, "and better. Somehow he gets thoughtful sitting by himself so much, and thinks the strangest things you ever heard. He told me, coming home, that he hoped the people saw him in the church, because he was a cripple, and it might be pleasant to them to remember upon Christmas Day, who made lame beggars walk and blind men see." [28]

Bob's voice was tremulous when he told them this, and trembled more when he said that Tiny Tim was growing strong and hearty.

His active little crutch was heard upon the floor, and back came Tiny Tim before another word was spoken, escorted by his brother and sister to his stool beside the fire; and while Bob, turning up his cuffs—as if, poor fellow, they were capable of being made more shabby—compounded some hot mixture in a jug with gin and lemons, and stirred it round and round and put it on the hob to simmer; Master Peter and the two ubiquitous young Cratchits went to fetch the goose, with which they soon returned in high procession.

Such a bustle ensued that you might have thought a goose the rarest of all birds; a feathered phenomenon, to which a black swan was a matter of course: and in truth it was something very like it in that house. Mrs. Cratchit made the gravy (ready beforehand in a little saucepan) hissing hot; Master Peter mashed the potatoes with incredible vigour; Miss Belinda sweetened up

[27] The *copper* was the boiler, usually used for washing laundry—which is why it is located in the "wash-house" and also why the Christmas pudding is said to produce a "smell like a washing-day."

[28] Dickens references two of the healing miracles of Jesus—the lame beggar whom Christ told to walk in John 5:1-9 and the blind man whom Christ told to see in Mark 8:22-25.

[29] Originally, the family was more formal—"all stood up while Bob said grace."

[30] In one *Carol* play, a real meal was served at the Cratchits'. The actress playing Tiny Tim was feeding her poor family with bits of the dinner. Hearing this, Dickens said, "You ought to have given her the whole goose."

[31] Dickens slightly sours the scene of goodwill with a reminder that selfishness never ceases—for it was a sadly ironic fact that, even on Christmas Day, when most thought more of giving than getting, in the neighborhoods of the poor, as elsewhere, theft was an ever-present threat.

the apple-sauce; Martha dusted the hot plates; Bob took Tiny Tim beside him in a tiny corner at the table; the two young Cratchits set chairs for everybody, not forgetting themselves, and mounting guard upon their posts, crammed spoons into their mouths, lest they should shriek for goose before their turn came to be helped. At last the dishes were set on, and grace was said. [29] It was succeeded by a breathless pause, as Mrs. Cratchit, looking slowly all along the carving-knife, prepared to plunge it in the breast; but when she did, and when the long expected gush of stuffing issued forth, one murmur of delight arose all round the board, and even Tiny Tim, excited by the two young Cratchits, beat on the table with the handle of his knife, and feebly cried Hurrah!

There never was such a goose. Bob said he didn't believe there ever was such a goose cooked. Its tenderness and flavour, size and cheapness, were the themes of universal admiration. Eked out by apple-sauce and mashed potatoes, it was a sufficient dinner for the whole family; indeed, as Mrs. Cratchit said with great delight (surveying one small atom of a bone upon the dish), they hadn't ate it all at last! Yet every one had had enough, and the youngest Cratchits in particular, were steeped in sage and onion to the eyebrows! [30] But now, the plates being changed by Miss Belinda, Mrs. Cratchit left the room alone—too nervous to bear witnesses—to take the pudding up, and bring it in.

Suppose it should not be done enough! Suppose it should break in turning out! Suppose somebody should have got over the wall of the back-yard, and stolen it, [31] while they were merry with the goose: a supposition at which the two young Cratchits became livid! All sorts of horrors were supposed.

Hallo! A great deal of steam! The pudding was out of the copper. A smell like a washing-day! That was the cloth. A smell like an eating-house, and a pastry cook's next door to each other, with a laundress's next door to that! That was the pudding! In half a minute Mrs. Cratchit entered: flushed, but smiling proudly: with the pudding, like a speckled cannon-ball, so hard and firm, blazing in half of half-a-quartern of ignited brandy, and bedight with Christmas holly stuck into the top.

Oh, a wonderful pudding! Bob Cratchit said, and calmly too, that he regarded it as the greatest success achieved by Mrs. Cratchit since their marriage. Mrs. Cratchit said that now the weight was off her mind, she would confess she had had her doubts about the quantity of flour. Everybody had something to say about it, but nobody said or thought it was at all a small pudding for a large family. It would have been flat heresy to do so. Any Cratchit would have blushed to hint at such a thing.

At last the dinner was all done, the cloth was cleared, the hearth swept, and the fire made up. The compound in the jug being tasted and considered perfect, apples and oranges were put upon the table, and a shovel-full of chesnuts on the fire. Then all the Cratchit family drew round the hearth, in what Bob Cratchit called a circle, meaning half a one; and at Bob Cratchit's elbow stood the family display of glass; two tumblers, and a custard-cup without a handle.

These held the hot stuff from the jug, however, as well as golden goblets would have done; and Bob served it out with beaming looks, while the chesnuts on the fire sputtered and crackled noisily. Then Bob proposed:

"A Merry Christmas to us all, my dears. God bless us!"

Which all the family re-echoed.

"God bless us every one!" [32] said Tiny Tim, the last of all.

He sat very close to his father's side, upon his little stool. Bob held his withered little hand in his, as if he loved the child, and wished to keep him by his side, and dreaded that he might be taken from him.

"Spirit," said Scrooge, with an interest he had never felt before, "tell me if Tiny Tim will live."

"I see a vacant seat," [33] replied the Ghost, "in the poor chimney corner, and a crutch without an owner, carefully preserved. If these shadows remain unaltered by the Future, [34] the child will die."

"No, no," said Scrooge. "Oh no, kind Spirit! say he will be spared."

"If these shadows remain unaltered by the Future, none other of my race," returned the Ghost, "will find him here. What then? If he be like to die, he had better do it, and decrease the surplus population." [35]

Scrooge hung his head to hear his own words quoted by the Spirit, and was overcome with penitence [36] and grief.

"Man," said the Ghost, "if man you be in heart, not adamant, forbear that wicked cant until you have discovered What the surplus is, and Where it is. Will you decide what men shall live, what men shall die? It may be, that in the sight of Heaven, you are more worthless and less fit to live than millions like this poor man's child. Oh God! to hear the Insect on the leaf pronouncing on the too much life among his hungry brothers in the dust!"

Scrooge bent before the Ghost's rebuke, and trembling cast his eyes upon the ground. [37] But he raised them speedily, on hearing his own name.

"Mr. Scrooge!" said Bob; "I'll give you Mr. Scrooge, the Founder of the Feast!"

"The Founder of the Feast indeed!" cried Mrs. Cratchit, reddening. "I wish I had him here. I'd give him a piece of my mind to feast upon, and I hope he'd have a good appetite for it."

"My dear," said Bob, "the children; Christmas Day."

"It should be Christmas Day, I am sure," said she, "on which one drinks the health of such an odious, stingy, hard, unfeeling man as Mr. Scrooge. You know he is, Robert! Nobody knows it better than you do, poor fellow!"

"My dear," was Bob's mild answer, "Christmas Day."

"I'll drink his health for your sake and the Day's," said Mrs. Cratchit, "not for his. Long life to him! A merry Christmas and a happy new year!—he'll be very merry and very happy, I have no doubt!" [38]

The children drank the toast after her. It was the first of their proceedings which had no heartiness in it. Tiny Tim drank it last of all, but he didn't care twopence for it. Scrooge was the Ogre of the family. The mention of his name cast a dark shadow on the party, which was not dispelled for full five minutes.

After it had passed away, they were ten times merrier than before, from the mere relief of Scrooge the Baleful being done with. Bob Cratchit told them how he had a situation in his eye for Master Peter, which would bring in, if obtained, full five-and-sixpence weekly. The two young Cratchits laughed tremendously at the idea of Peter's being a man of business; and Peter himself looked thoughtfully at the fire from between his collars, as if he were deliberating what particular investments he should favour when he came into the receipt of that bewildering income. Martha, who was a poor apprentice at a

[38] Dickens presents a paradigm of Christian living—as Bob shows not only forgiveness but goodwill toward his offender, which is set against the unforgiving ill-will of his wife, however justified, with his good example finally affecting her for the better.

milliner's, then told them what kind of work she had to do, and how many hours she worked at a stretch, and how she meant to lie a-bed to-morrow morning for a good long rest; to-morrow being a holiday she passed at home. Also how she had seen a countess and a lord some days before, and how the lord "was much about as tall as Peter;" at which Peter pulled up his collars so high that you couldn't have seen his head if you had been there. All this time the chesnuts and the jug went round and round; and bye and bye they had a song, about a lost child travelling in the snow, from Tiny Tim; who had a plaintive little voice, and sang it very well indeed.

There was nothing of high mark in this. They were not a handsome family; they were not well dressed; their shoes were far from being waterproof; their clothes were scanty; and Peter might have known, and very likely did, the inside of a pawnbroker's. [39] But they were happy, grateful, pleased with one another, and contented with the time; and when they faded, and looked happier yet in the bright sprinklings of the Spirit's torch at parting, Scrooge had his eye upon them, and especially on Tiny Tim, until the last.

By this time it was getting dark, and snowing pretty heavily; and as Scrooge and the Spirit went along the streets, the brightness of the roaring fires in kitchens, parlours, and all sorts of rooms, was wonderful. Here, the flickering of the blaze showed preparations for a cosy dinner, with hot plates baking through and through before the fire, and deep red curtains, ready to be drawn, to shut out cold and darkness. There, all the children of the house were running out into the snow to meet their married sisters, brothers, cousins, uncles, aunts, and be the first to greet them. Here, again, were shadows on the window-blind of guests

[39] Unfortunately, young Dickens did too (see Stave Two, Note 19).

assembling; and there a group of handsome girls, all hooded and fur-booted, and all chattering at once, tripped lightly off to some near neighbour's house; where, woe upon the single man who saw them enter—artful witches: well they knew it—in a glow!

But if you had judged from the numbers of people on their way to friendly gatherings, you might have thought that no one was at home to give them welcome when they got there, instead of every house expecting company, and piling up its fires half-chimney high. Blessings on it, how the Ghost exulted! How it bared its breadth of breast, and opened its capacious palm, and floated on, outpouring, with a generous hand, its bright and harmless mirth on everything within its reach! The very lamplighter, who ran on before dotting the dusky street with specks of light, and who was dressed to spend the evening somewhere, laughed out loudly as the Spirit passed: though little kenned the lamplighter that he had any company but Christmas!

And now, without a word of warning from the Ghost, they stood upon a bleak and desert moor, where monstrous masses of rude stone were cast about, as though it were the burial-place of giants; and water spread itself wheresoever it listed— or would have done so, but for the frost that held it prisoner; and nothing grew but moss and furze, and coarse, rank grass. Down in the west the setting sun had left a streak of fiery red, which glared upon the desolation for an instant, like a sullen eye, and frowning lower, lower, lower yet, was lost in the thick gloom of darkest night.

"What place is this?" asked Scrooge.

"A place where Miners live, who labour in the bowels of the earth," [40] returned the Spirit. "But they know me. See!"

[40] The Spirit has brought Scrooge to Cornwall, England, a place Dickens was moved to visit in the fall of 1842 after he had read a recent report about the state of child labor in the Cornish mines.

A light shone from the window of a hut, and swiftly they advanced towards it. Passing through the wall of mud and stone, they found a cheerful company assembled round a glowing fire. An old, old man and woman, with their children and their children's children, and another generation beyond that, all decked out gaily in their holiday attire. The old man, in a voice that seldom rose above the howling of the wind upon the barren waste, was singing them a Christmas song; it had been a very old song when he was a boy; [41] and from time to time they all joined in the chorus. So surely as they raised their voices, the old man got quite blithe and loud; and so surely as they stopped, his vigour sank again.

[41] Cornwall is renowned for its Christmas carols, some of which are over three hundred years old.

The Spirit did not tarry here, but bade Scrooge hold his robe, and passing on above the moor, sped whither? Not to sea? To sea. To Scrooge's horror, looking back, he saw the last of the land, a frightful range of rocks, behind them; and his ears were deafened by the thundering of water, as it rolled, and roared, and raged among the dreadful caverns it had worn, and fiercely tried to undermine the earth.

Built upon a dismal reef of sunken rocks, some league or so from shore, on which the waters chafed and dashed, the wild year through, there stood a solitary lighthouse. Great heaps of sea-weed clung to its base, and storm-birds—born of the wind one might suppose, as sea-weed of the water—rose and fell about it, like the waves they skimmed.

But even here, two men who watched the light had made a fire, that through the loophole in the thick stone wall shed out a ray of brightness on the awful sea. Joining their horny hands over the rough table at which they sat, they wished each other Merry Christmas in their can of grog; and one of them: the elder, too, with his face all damaged and scarred with hard weather, as the figure-head of an old ship might be: struck up a sturdy song that was like a Gale in itself. [42]

Again the Ghost sped on, above the black and heaving sea—on, on—until, being far away, as he told Scrooge, from any shore, they lighted on a ship. They stood beside the helmsman at the wheel, the look-out in the bow, the officers who had the watch; dark, ghostly figures in their several stations; but every man among them hummed a Christmas tune, or had a Christmas thought, or spoke below his breath to his companion of some bygone Christmas Day, with homeward hopes belonging to it. And every man on board, waking or sleeping, good or bad, had had a kinder word for another on that day than on any day in the year; and had shared to some extent in its festivities; and had remembered those he cared for at a distance, and had known that they delighted to remember him.

It was a great surprise to Scrooge, while listening to the moaning of the wind, and thinking what a solemn thing it was to move on through the lonely darkness over an unknown abyss, whose depths were secrets as profound as Death: it was a great surprise to Scrooge, while thus engaged, to hear a hearty laugh. It was a much greater surprise to Scrooge to recognise it as his own nephew's, and to find himself in a bright, dry, gleaming room, with the Spirit standing smiling by his side, and looking at that same nephew with approving affability!

"Ha, ha!" laughed Scrooge's nephew. "Ha, ha, ha!"

If you should happen, by any unlikely chance, to know a man more blest in a laugh than Scrooge's nephew, all I can say is, I should like to know him too. Introduce him to me, and I'll cultivate his acquaintance.

It is a fair, even-handed, noble adjustment of things, that while there is infection in disease and sor-

[42] While Scrooge did not know the spirit of Christmas, although he was "rich enough" (per his nephew), these lowly Cornish workers "know" the Spirit of Christmas (per the Spirit), despite their circumstances, whether physical, financial, or otherwise.

row, there is nothing in the world so irresistibly conta-
gious as laughter and good-humour. When Scrooge's
nephew laughed in this way: holding his sides, rolling
his head, and twisting his face into the most extrav-
agant contortions: Scrooge's niece, by marriage,
laughed as heartily as he. And their assembled friends
being not a bit behindhand, roared out lustily.

"Ha, ha! Ha, ha, ha, ha!"

"He said that Christmas was a humbug, as I live!"
cried Scrooge's nephew. "He believed it too!"

"More shame for him, Fred!" [43] said Scrooge's
niece, indignantly. Bless those women; they never do
anything by halves. They are always in earnest.

She was very pretty: exceedingly pretty. With a
dimpled, surprised-looking, capital face; a ripe little
mouth, that seemed made to be kissed—as no doubt
it was; all kinds of good little dots about her chin,
that melted into one another when she laughed; and
the sunniest pair of eyes you ever saw in any little
creature's head. Altogether she was what you would
have called provoking, you know; but satisfactory,
too. Oh, perfectly satisfactory.

"He's a comical old fellow," said Scrooge's
nephew, "that's the truth; and not so pleasant as he
might be. However, his offences carry their own punishment, and I have nothing to say against him."

"I'm sure he is very rich, Fred," hinted Scrooge's
niece. "At least you always tell *me* so."

"What of that, my dear!" said Scrooge's nephew.
"His wealth is of no use to him. He don't do any
good with it. He don't make himself comfortable
with it. He hasn't the satisfaction of thinking—ha, ha,
ha!—that he is ever going to benefit Us with it."

"I have no patience with him," observed
Scrooge's niece. Scrooge's niece's sisters, and all the
other ladies, expressed the same opinion.

[43] Dickens finally reveals the nephew's "Christian name."

"Oh, I have!" said Scrooge's nephew. "I am sorry for him; I couldn't be angry with him if I tried. [44] Who suffers by his ill whims! Himself, always. Here, he takes it into his head to dislike us, and he won't come and dine with us. What's the consequence? He don't lose much of a dinner."

"Indeed, I think he loses a very good dinner," interrupted Scrooge's niece. Everybody else said the same, and they must be allowed to have been competent judges, because they had just had dinner; and, with the dessert upon the table, were clustered round the fire, by lamplight.

"Well! I am very glad to hear it," said Scrooge's nephew, "because I haven't any great faith in these young housekeepers. What do *you* say, Topper?"

Topper had clearly got his eye upon one of Scrooge's niece's sisters, for he answered that a bachelor was a wretched outcast, who had no right to express an opinion on the subject. Whereat Scrooge's niece's sister—the plump one with the lace tucker: not the one with the roses—blushed.

"Do go on, Fred," said Scrooge's niece, clapping her hands. "He never finishes what he begins to say! He is such a ridiculous fellow!"

Scrooge's nephew revelled in another laugh, and as it was impossible to keep the infection off; though the plump sister tried hard to do it with aromatic vinegar; his example was unanimously followed.

"I was only going to say," said Scrooge's nephew, "that the consequence of his taking a dislike to us, and not making merry with us, is, as I think, that he loses some pleasant moments, which could do him no harm. I am sure he loses pleasanter companions than he can find in his own thoughts, either in his mouldy old office, or his dusty chambers. I mean to give him the same chance every year, whether he

[44] Dickens presents a second paradigm of Christian living—as Fred and his wife parallel Bob Cratchit and his wife (see Note 38), with Fred offering forgiveness and goodwill toward Scrooge in contrast to the unforgiving ill-will of his wife. Here, however, Fred goes farther in detailing the un-Christian attitude of his uncle and its self-punishing consequence.

[45] Rather than thinking of how his kindness might benefit himself, true to the "Carol Philosophy" (see Stave One, Note 18), Fred thinks of how his kindness might benefit another.

[46] A "Glee" is a musical composition for three or more parts and a "Catch" is a kind of musical round for three or more parts in which each is singing a different line at the same time.

[47] This passage, "it is good to be children sometimes, and never better than at Christmas, when its mighty Founder was a child himself," sparked controversy on its publication, drawing both praise and condemnation from religious readers for its direct (and therefore some said irreverent) reference to the Christ of Christmas.

likes it or not, for I pity him. He may rail at Christmas till he dies, but he can't help thinking better of it—I defy him—if he finds me going there, in good temper, year after year, and saying Uncle Scrooge, how are you? If it only puts him in the vein to leave his poor clerk fifty pounds, [45] *that's* something; and I think I shook him yesterday."

It was their turn to laugh now, at the notion of his shaking Scrooge. But being thoroughly good-natured, and not much caring what they laughed at, so that they laughed at any rate, he encouraged them in their merriment, and passed the bottle, joyously.

After tea, they had some music. For they were a musical family, and knew what they were about, when they sung a Glee or Catch, [46] I can assure you: especially Topper, who could growl away in the bass like a good one, and never swell the large veins in his forehead, or get red in the face over it. Scrooge's niece played well upon the harp; and played among other tunes a simple little air (a mere nothing: you might learn to whistle it in two minutes), which had been familiar to the child who fetched Scrooge from the boarding-school, as he had been reminded by the Ghost of Christmas Past. When this strain of music sounded, all the things that Ghost had shown him, came upon his mind; he softened more and more; and thought that if he could have listened to it often, years ago, he might have cultivated the kindnesses of life for his own happiness with his own hands, without resorting to the sexton's spade that buried Jacob Marley.

But they didn't devote the whole evening to music. After a while they played at forfeits; for it is good to be children sometimes, and never better than at Christmas, when its mighty Founder was a child himself. [47] Stop! There was first a game at blindman's buff. Of course there was. And I no more believe Topper was really blind than I believe he had eyes in his boots. My opinion is, that it was a done thing between him and Scrooge's nephew; and that the Ghost of Christmas Present knew it. The way he went after that plump sister in the lace tucker, was an outrage on the credulity of human nature. Knocking down the fire-irons, tumbling over the chairs, bumping against the piano, smothering himself among the curtains, wherever she went, there went he. He always knew where the plump sister was. He wouldn't catch anybody else. If you had fallen up against him, as some of them did, and stood there; he would have made a feint of endeavouring to seize you, which would have been an affront to your understanding; and would instantly have sidled off in the direction of the plump sister. She often cried out that it wasn't fair; and it really was not. But when at last, he caught her; when, in spite of all her silken rustlings, and her rapid flutterings past him, he got her into a corner whence there was no escape; then his conduct was the most execrable. For his pretending not to know her; his pretending that it was necessary to touch her head-dress, and further to assure himself of her identity by pressing a certain ring upon her finger, and a certain chain about her neck; was vile, monstrous! No doubt she told him her opinion of it, when, another blind-man being in office, they were so very confidential together, behind the curtains.

Scrooge's niece was not one of the blind-man's buff party, but was made comfortable with a large chair and a footstool, in a snug corner, where the Ghost and Scrooge were close behind her. But she joined in the forfeits, and loved her love to admiration with all the letters of the alphabet. Likewise at the game of How, When, and Where, she was very great, and to the secret joy of Scrooge's nephew, beat her sisters hollow: though they were sharp girls too, as Topper could have told you. There might have been twenty people there, young and old, but they all played, and so did Scrooge; for, wholly forgetting in the interest he had in what was going on, that his voice made no sound in their ears, he sometimes came out with his guess quite loud, and very often guessed right, too; for the sharpest needle, best Whitechapel, [48] warranted not to cut in the eye, was not sharper than Scrooge: blunt as he took it in his head to be.

[48] Whitechapel is an area in East London where there were needle factories. The name of the district was applied to a certain kind of needle.

The Ghost was greatly pleased to find him in this mood, and looked upon him with such favour that he begged like a boy to be allowed to stay until the guests departed. But this the Spirit said could not be done.

"Here's a new game," said Scrooge. "One half hour, Spirit, only one!"

It was a Game called Yes and No, where Scrooge's nephew had to think of something, and the rest must find out what; he only answering to their questions yes or no as the case was. The brisk fire of questioning to which he was exposed, elicited from him that he was thinking of an animal, a live animal, rather a disagreeable animal, a savage animal, an animal that growled and grunted sometimes, and talked sometimes, and lived in London, and walked about the streets, and wasn't made a show of, and wasn't led by anybody, and didn't live in a menagerie, and was never killed in a market, and was not a horse, or an ass, or a cow, or a bull, or a tiger, or a dog, or a pig, or a cat, or a bear. At every fresh question that was put to him, this nephew burst into a fresh roar of laughter; and was so inexpressibly tickled, that he was obliged to get up off the sofa and stamp. At last the plump sister, falling into a similar state, cried out:

"I have found it out! I know what it is, Fred! I know what it is!"

"What is it?" cried Fred.

"It's your Uncle Scro-o-o-oge!"

Which it certainly was. Admiration was the universal sentiment, though some objected that the reply to "Is it a bear?" ought to have been "Yes;" inasmuch as an answer in the negative was sufficient to have diverted their thoughts from Mr. Scrooge, supposing they had ever had any tendency that way.

"He has given us plenty of merriment, I am sure," said Fred, "and it would be ungrateful not to drink his health. Here is a glass of mulled wine ready to our hand at the moment; and I say, 'Uncle Scrooge!'"

"Well! Uncle Scrooge!" they cried.

"A Merry Christmas and a happy New Year to the old man, whatever he is!" said Scrooge's nephew. "He wouldn't take it from me, but may he have it, nevertheless. Uncle Scrooge!"

Uncle Scrooge had imperceptibly become so gay and light of heart, that he would have pledged the unconscious company in return, and thanked them in an inaudible speech, if the Ghost had given him time. But the whole scene passed off in the breath of the last word spoken by his nephew; and he and the Spirit were again upon their travels.

Much they saw, and far they went, and many homes they visited, but always with a happy end. The Spirit stood beside sick beds, and they were cheerful; on foreign lands, and they were close at home; by struggling men, and they were patient in their greater hope; by poverty, and it was rich. [49] In almshouse, hospital, and jail, in misery's every refuge, where vain man in his little brief authority [50] had not made fast the door, and barred the Spirit out, he left his blessing, and taught Scrooge his precepts.

It was a long night, if it were only a night; but Scrooge had his doubts of this, because the Christ-

[49] Dickens has his Spirit of Christmas portray the spirit of Christianity, as he wrote in *The Life of Our Lord*, "Remember!—It is Christianity TO DO GOOD, always—even to those who do evil to us. It is Christianity to love our neighbor as ourself, and to do to all men as we would have them do to us. It is Christianity to be gentle, merciful, and forgiving, and to keep those qualities quiet in our own hearts."

[50] Dickens refers to Shakespeare—no stranger to the Bible with as many as 2,000 scriptural references across thirty-seven plays—alluding to *Measure for Measure*, Act II, Scene 2, lines 117-122: "But man, proud man,/ Drest in a little brief authority,/ Most ignorant of what he's most assured,/ His glassy essence, like an angry ape,/ Plays such fantastic tricks before high heaven,/ As make the angels weep."

[51] In London at this time, the Holidays stretched from Christmas Day until Epiphany on January 6th, twelve days in all.

[52] Dickens greatly enjoyed celebrating the Twelfth Night as part of the festivities for his son's birthday ("Charley") each year. Many children were invited to the Dickenses' home, and the author was known to delight his young audiences with magic tricks on more than one such occasion.

[53] Through the demon children Ignorance and Want, Dickens makes both a spiritual plea to turn from the sin of apathy and a physical plea to provide for impoverished children.

mas Holidays [51] appeared to be condensed into the space of time they passed together. It was strange, too, that while Scrooge remained unaltered in his outward form, the Ghost grew older, clearly older. Scrooge had observed this change, but never spoke of it, until they left a children's Twelfth Night party, [52] when, looking at the Spirit as they stood together in an open place, he noticed that its hair was gray.

"Are spirits' lives so short?" asked Scrooge.

"My life upon this globe, is very brief," replied the Ghost. "It ends to-night."

"To-night!" cried Scrooge.

"To-night at midnight. Hark! The time is drawing near."

The chimes were ringing the three quarters past eleven at that moment.

"Forgive me if I am not justified in what I ask," said Scrooge, looking intently at the Spirit's robe, "but I see something strange, and not belonging to yourself, protruding from your skirts. Is it a foot or a claw!"

"It might be a claw, for the flesh there is upon it," was the Spirit's sorrowful reply. "Look here."

From the foldings of its robe, it brought two children; wretched, abject, frightful, hideous, miserable. They knelt down at its feet, and clung upon the outside of its garment. [53]

"Oh, Man! look here. Look, look, down here!" exclaimed the Ghost.

They were a boy and girl. Yellow, meagre, ragged, scowling, wolfish; but prostrate, too, in their humility. Where graceful youth should have filled their features out, and touched them with its freshest tints, a stale and shrivelled hand, like that of age, had pinched, and twisted them, and pulled them into shreds. Where angels might have sat enthroned, devils lurked, and glared out menacing. No change, no degradation, no perversion of humanity, in any grade, through all the mysteries of wonderful creation, has monsters half so horrible and dread. [54]

Scrooge started back, appalled. Having them shown to him in this way, he tried to say they were fine children, but the words choked themselves, rather than be parties to a lie of such enormous magnitude.

"Spirit! are they yours?" Scrooge could say no more.

"They are Man's," said the Spirit, looking down upon them. "And they cling to me, appealing from their fathers. [55] This boy is Ignorance. This girl is Want. [56] Beware them both, and all of their degree, but most of all beware this boy, for on his brow I see that written which is Doom, unless the writing be erased. Deny it!" cried the Spirit, stretching out its hand towards the city. "Slander those who tell it ye! Admit it for your factious purposes, and make it worse. And bide the end!"

"Have they no refuge or resource?" cried Scrooge.

"Are there no prisons?" said the Spirit, turning on him for the last time with his own words. "Are there no workhouses?"

The bell struck twelve. [57]

Scrooge looked about him for the Ghost, and saw it not. As the last stroke ceased to vibrate, he remembered the prediction of old Jacob Marley, and lifting up his eyes, beheld a solemn Phantom, draped and hooded, coming, like a mist along the ground, towards him.

[54] Dickens himself had been one of these children, when at the age of twelve, with his family in debt, the boy was taken out of school to search for work. Of this time, Dickens later wrote in his somewhat autobiographical novel, *David Copperfield*, "I know I do not exaggerate, consciously and unintentionally, the scantiness of my resources and the difficulties of my life."

[55] In public readings, Dickens changed the poetic "their fathers" to the less fanciful—and more convicting—"mankind." The Spirit cares for these children because "mankind" will not.

[56] About such ignorance and want, again in *David Copperfield* Dickens wrote, "I know that I have lounged about the streets, insufficiently and unsatisfactorily fed. I know that, but for the mercy of God, I might easily have been, for any care that was taken of me, a little robber or a little vagabond."

[57] Dickens uses "twelve" to recall both the last hour of the day and the last day of Christmastime. Unlike the two previous Spirits who came at one o'clock, the first hour of a new day, this Spirit, like death, comes at the last hour of the last day.

Repentance

I. TELLING THE STORY

While in Stave Two we saw Scrooge feeling sorry for the shadows of his past self, it's in Stave Three that we see him begin to change in the present, and watch him even as he learns how to do that. The Ghost of Christmas Present shows the cynical man how Christmas is truly kept: revealing to the old miser people with empty hands, but generous hearts; people in lowly conditions, who yet rejoice; people who lack material wealth, and still are rich in family and friends. Through these scenes, and the feelings that come with them, Ebenezer's regrets bring him to repentance.

Key Verse

"Godly sorrow brings repentance that leads to salvation and leaves no regret, but worldly sorrow brings death."
—2 CORINTHIANS 7:10

A. When Scrooge meets the Ghost of Christmas Present, he tells him, "I learnt a lesson which is working now." What lesson do you think Scrooge was talking about?

B. As Scrooge watches the Cratchits, he asks the Spirit, "with an interest he had never felt before," if Tiny Tim will live. How does the Ghost hint that Scrooge could change the boy's future?

C. "Much they saw, and far they went, and many homes they visited, but always with a happy end." The story tells us that in all the places the Spirit took Scrooge, "he left his blessing, and taught Scrooge his precepts." From what the story tells us about where they went and what they saw, what do you think are the precepts, or principles, of the Ghost of Christmas Present? How might these precepts have helped Scrooge come to repentance?

D. Twice in Stave Three the Spirit confronts Scrooge with his own words. And in the scene from his nephew's house, Scrooge is again made to hear words he had uttered and to see his former attitude through other's eyes. In each of these instances, how does Scrooge appear different from when we first heard him say those words? What changes does the author allow us to see in the character's mind and heart?

II. TELLING YOUR STORY

Repentance means admitting we were wrong, and then doing something about it. When confronted with our sins, too often we respond by becoming prideful and defensive, trying to cover up for what we've done. However, it is impossible to repent from a mistake you do not admit you made. Hiding our sins may be a natural human reaction, but it offers us no real benefit because it dooms us to repeat our mistakes. Rather than repeat, we should repent.

Key Verse

"If we confess our sins, he is faithful and just and will forgive us our sins and purify us from all unrighteousness. If we claim we have not sinned, we make him out to be a liar and his word has no place in our lives."

—1 JOHN 1:9, 10

A. The last time you did something wrong, what did you about it? Did you try to hide it, or did you ask for forgiveness? Was it easy or hard to do what you did? Why?

When Scrooge saw how he could make a difference in people's lives (such as that of Tiny Tim), he wanted to change. What is something that has made you want to change the way you act? How do you think that helps you to repent?

C. When at his nephew's house Scrooge heard a certain strain of music that his sister used to play, he "thought that if he could have listened to it often, years ago, he might have cultivated the kindnesses of life for his own happiness with his own hands." What in your life helps you to cultivate kindness? What have you had to overcome to learn repentance?

D. When Scrooge is faced with the children named Want and Ignorance, he is appalled by these "monsters" so "horrible and dread." The words and even the concepts of want and ignorance may not sound so terrible to us—perhaps we would replace these characters with murder or greed, or something else. Why do you think Dickens chose these two? What ugliness do you need to face in order to make a difference in your life or the world around you?

III. Telling the Story of Christmas

The Israelites had been waiting a long time for their Messiah to come. But when Jesus came, he was not the warrior king some imagined would save their people. Instead, he spent his life often among the poor, the lowly, and among sinners like you and me. Even from the beginning, he brought God's message of forgiveness and love in unexpected ways. And he calls us all now to repent and follow his example of an uncommon life.

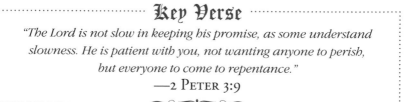

Key Verse

"The Lord is not slow in keeping his promise, as some understand slowness. He is patient with you, not wanting anyone to perish, but everyone to come to repentance."

—2 Peter 3:9

A. As we read in Luke 2, when the angel first came to the shepherds as they watched over their flocks, they were terrified. But they listened to the message, immediately believed, and went to see the baby Jesus. Shepherds were not important or powerful people in the first century. Why do you think God shared the news of the birth of his son with them first?

B. When they had seen the baby in the manger, the shepherds "spread the word concerning what had been told them about this child" (Luke 2:17). Scrooge's nephew had decided to keep trying to bring the message of Christmas to the old man year after year, even if he kept rejecting him. Think of someone you need to tell about Jesus. How do you think you can best spread this message? What will help you keep trying?

C. When Mrs. Cratchit speaks poorly of Scrooge, Bob reminds her, "Christmas Day." The Spirit promotes this same feeling, stopping quarrels and spreading goodwill wherever he goes. What do you think it is about Christmas that makes people want to behave better and be more forgiving than at other times of the year? How do you think you might spread this feeling all year round?

D. To give us all a chance to repent, God has patiently postponed his wrath. But the day of judgment will come. In the meantime, God has sent us another message: "Produce fruit in keeping with repentance" (Matthew 3:8). Fruit is a product of growth and a seed for growth. The shepherds returned to take care of their sheep, but they were glorifying and praising God. In what ways can you produce fruit in your life and by so doing, glorify God? How can you tell when someone is truly repentant?

IV. LIVING THE STORY

When we are repentant, we show God that we know we have sinned, we confess our sins to him, and we acknowledge that we need his power to change. And God is faithful, as he tells his prophet in Jeremiah 15:19, "If you repent, I will restore you that you may serve me." Once we are willing to admit our sin and commit to change, we can be a fruitful member of God's kingdom.

Ask God to help you practice repentance by:

✦ Giving you the ability to see your sin clearly and honestly.

✦ Giving you the heart to want to change.

✦ Giving you courage to ask and give forgiveness.

For Further Study

Job 42:5, 6

Proverbs 28:13, 14

Jeremiah 15:19

Matthew 6:12-15

Luke 5:31, 32

Acts 2:36-39; 17:29-31

Romans 2:1-9

The Last of the Spirits

The Phantom slowly, gravely, silently, approached. When it came near him, Scrooge bent down upon his knee; [1] for in the very air through which this Spirit moved it seemed to scatter gloom and mystery.

It was shrouded in a deep black [2] garment, which concealed its head, its face, its form, and left nothing of it visible save one outstretched hand. But for this it would have been difficult to detach its figure from the night, and separate it from the darkness by which it was surrounded. [3]

He felt that it was tall and stately when it came beside him, and that its mysterious presence filled him with a solemn dread. He knew no more, for the Spirit neither spoke nor moved.

"I am in the presence of the Ghost of Christmas Yet To Come?" said Scrooge.

The Spirit answered not, but pointed onward with its hand.

"You are about to show me shadows of the things that have not happened, but will happen in the time before us," Scrooge pursued. "Is that so, Spirit?"

The upper portion of the garment was contracted

[1] In kneeling, Scrooge resumes a penitential posture, reminding us, after so much merrymaking, of where he is on his spiritual journey— from sinful, to regretful, to repentant, but not yet saved.

[2] To color the third Spirit, Dickens uses black, the color used often in the Bible and elsewhere to symbolize death.

[3] The specter of death is a harsh but familiar phantom at Christmas, when we recall lost loved ones and remember the Savior who was born to die, that they may live again.

for an instant in its folds, as if the Spirit had inclined its head. That was the only answer he received.

Although well used to ghostly company by this time, Scrooge feared the silent shape so much that his legs trembled beneath him, and he found that he could hardly stand when he prepared to follow it. The Spirit paused a moment, as observing his condition, and giving him time to recover.

But Scrooge was all the worse for this. It thrilled him with a vague uncertain horror, to know that behind the dusky shroud there were ghostly eyes intently fixed upon him, while he, though he stretched his own to the utmost, could see nothing but a spectral hand and one great heap of black.

"Ghost of the Future!" he exclaimed, "I fear you more than any Spectre I have seen. But, as I know your purpose is to do me good, and as I hope [4] to live to be another man from what I was, I am prepared to bear you company, and do it with a thankful heart. Will you not speak to me?"

[4] This is a hope new to Scrooge, but central to the lives of Christians—the hope of salvation.

It gave him no reply. The hand was pointed straight before them.

"Lead on!" said Scrooge. "Lead on! The night is waning fast, and it is precious time to me, I know. Lead on, Spirit!"

The Phantom moved away as it had come towards him. Scrooge followed in the shadow of its dress, which bore him up, he thought, and carried him along.

They scarcely seemed to enter the city; for the city rather seemed to spring up about them, and encompass them of its own act. But there they were, in the heart of it; on 'Change, amongst the merchants; who hurried up and down, and chinked the money in their pockets, and conversed in groups, and looked at their watches, and trifled thoughtfully with their great gold seals; and so forth, as Scrooge had seen them often.

The Spirit stopped beside one little knot of business men. Observing that the hand was pointed to them, Scrooge advanced to listen to their talk.

"No," said a great fat man with a monstrous chin, "I don't know much about it, either way. I only know he's dead."

"When did he die?" inquired another.

"Last night, I believe."

"Why, what was the matter with him?" asked a third, taking a vast quantity of snuff out of a very large snuff-box. "I thought he'd never die."

"God knows," said the first, with a yawn.

"What has he done with his money?" asked a red-faced gentleman with a pendulous excrescence on the end of his nose, that shook like the gills of a turkey-cock.

"I haven't heard," said the man with the large chin, yawning again. "Left it to his Company, perhaps. He hasn't left it to *me*. That's all I know." [5]

This pleasantry was received with a general laugh.

"It's likely to be a very cheap funeral," said the same speaker; "for upon my life I don't know of anybody to go to it. Suppose we make up a party and volunteer?"

"I don't mind going if a lunch is provided," observed the gentleman with the excrescence on his nose. "But I must be fed, if I make one."

Another laugh.

"Well, I am the most disinterested among you, after all," said the first speaker, "for I never wear black gloves, and I never eat lunch. But I'll offer to go, if anybody else will. When I come to think of it, I'm not at all sure that I wasn't his most particular friend; for

[5] In an earlier draft, Dickens added, "I wish he had," before removing the gratuitously greedy comment. We are back amongst the "Scrooges"—but Scrooge is no longer one of them.

[6] Dickens offers a doppel-ganger for Scrooge in all his ugly selfishness. This man is "disinterested" in paying his respects, despite being the deceased's "most particular friend," because of two trivial habits. The scene recalls the day of Marley's funeral, which Scrooge did not let go completely to waste, as he "solemnised it with an undoubted bargain."

[7] "Old Scratch" is a nick-name for the devil.

[8] A dark pun: *cold* de-scribes not only the weather, but their attitude toward the deceased.

we used to stop and speak whenever we met. Bye, bye!" [6]

Speakers and listeners strolled away, and mixed with other groups. Scrooge knew the men, and looked towards the Spirit for an explanation.

The Phantom glided on into a street. Its finger pointed to two persons meeting. Scrooge listened again, thinking that the explanation might lie here.

He knew these men, also, perfectly. They were men of business: very wealthy, and of great impor-tance. He had made a point always of standing well in their esteem: in a business point of view, that is; strictly in a business point of view.

"How are you?" said one.

"How are you?" returned the other.

"Well!" said the first. "Old Scratch [7] has got his own at last, hey?"

"So I am told," returned the second. "Cold, [8] isn't it?"

"Seasonable for Christmas time. You're not a skaiter, I suppose?"

"No. No. Something else to think of. Good morning!"

Not another word. That was their meeting, their conversation, and their parting.

Scrooge was at first inclined to be surprised that the Spirit should attach importance to conversations apparently so trivial; but feeling assured that they must have some hidden purpose, he set himself to con-sider what it was likely to be. They could scarcely be supposed to have any bearing on the death of Jacob, his old partner, for that was Past, and this Ghost's province was the Future. Nor could he think of any one immediately connected with himself, to whom he could apply them. But nothing doubting that to whomsoever they applied they had some latent moral for his own improvement, he resolved to treasure up every word he heard, and everything he saw; and especially to observe the shadow of himself when it appeared. For he had an expectation that the conduct of his future self would give him the clue he missed, and would render the solution of these riddles easy.

He looked about in that very place for his own image; but another man stood in his accustomed corner, and though the clock pointed to his usual time of day for being there, he saw no likeness of himself among the multitudes that poured in through the Porch. It gave him little surprise, however; for he had been revolving in his mind a change of life, and thought and hoped he saw his new-born resolutions carried out in this. [9]

Quiet and dark, beside him stood the Phantom, with its outstretched hand. When he roused himself from his thoughtful quest, he fancied from the turn of the hand, and its situation in reference to himself, that the Unseen Eyes were looking at him keenly. It made him shudder, and feel very cold.

They left the busy scene, and went into an obscure part of the town, where Scrooge had never penetrated before, although he recognised its situation, and its bad repute. The ways were foul and narrow; the shops and houses wretched; the people half-naked, drunken, slipshod, ugly. Alleys and archways, like so many cesspools, disgorged their offences of smell, and dirt, and life, upon the straggling streets; and the whole quarter reeked with crime, with filth, and misery. [10]

Far in this den of infamous resort, there was a low-browed, beetling shop, [11] below a pent-house roof, where iron, old rags, bottles, bones, and greasy offal, were bought. Upon the floor within, were piled up heaps of rusty keys, nails, chains, hinges, files, scales,

[9] Scrooge was blinded to his inner character before this; now he cannot see his external form. The author may wish to point out to us here that though Scrooge has begun to change his thoughts, his heart and actions have yet to fully follow. Ebenezer will have to do more yet before the Spirit can show him an altered Future, for "As the body without the spirit is dead, so faith without deeds is dead" (James 2:26).

[10] Having raised the specter of "Old Scratch," Dickens spares Scrooge (and the reader) a visit to the literal hell, descending instead to this symbolic hell-on-earth.

[11] *Beetling* means the shop projected out from the building. This type of shop, usually called a "rag-and-bottle shop," was a collection of miscellaneous items, something like a rather smelly, dirty, tightly packed garage sale. A fitting end, some might say, for a man who spent his life attaching a price to everything—that everything he has be sold for a price.

weights, and refuse iron of all kinds. Secrets that few would like to scrutinise were bred and hidden in mountains of unseemly rags, masses of corrupted fat, and sepulchres of bones. Sitting in among the wares he dealt in, by a charcoal stove, made of old bricks, was a gray-haired rascal, nearly seventy years of age; who had screened himself from the cold air without, by a frousy curtaining of miscellaneous tatters, hung upon a line; and smoked his pipe in all the luxury of calm retirement.

Scrooge and the Phantom came into the presence of this man, just as a woman with a heavy bundle slunk into the shop. But she had scarcely entered, when another woman, similarly laden, came in too; and she was closely followed by a man in faded black, who was no less startled by the sight of them, than they had been upon the recognition of each other. After a short period of blank astonishment, in which the old man with the pipe had joined them, they all three burst into a laugh. [12]

"Let the charwoman alone to be the first!" cried she who had entered first. "Let the laundress alone to be the second; and let the undertaker's man alone to be the third. Look here, old Joe, here's a chance! If we haven't all three met here without meaning it!"

"You couldn't have met in a better place," said old Joe, removing his pipe from his mouth. "Come into the parlour. You were made free of it long ago, you know; and the other two an't strangers. Stop till I shut the door of the shop. Ah! How it skreeks! There an't such a rusty bit of metal in the place as its own hinges, I believe; and I'm sure there's no such old bones here, as mine. Ha, ha! We're all suitable to our calling, we're well matched. Come into the parlour. Come into the parlour." [13]

The parlour was the space behind the screen of

[12] These three thieves are a grotesque parody of the three kings of the Christmas story, particularly in regard to the "charwoman" (house servant) and the "undertaker's man"—instead of heaven, they seem inspired by hell; instead of coming for a birth, they come from a death; and instead of gifts, they bear stolen items.

[13] In public readings, Dickens changed "Come into the parlour. Come into the parlour" to "What have you got to sell? What have you got to sell?" to announce that these three are here for mercenary purposes.

rags. The old man raked the fire together with an old stair-rod, and having trimmed his smoky lamp (for it was night), with the stem of his pipe, put it in his mouth again.

While he did this, the woman who had already spoken threw her bundle on the floor and sat down in a flaunting manner on a stool; crossing her elbows on her knees, and looking with a bold defiance at the other two.

"What odds then! What odds, Mrs. Dilber?" [14] said the woman. "Every person has a right to take care of themselves. *He* always did."

"That's true, indeed!" said the laundress. "No man more so."

"Why, then, don't stand staring as if you was afraid, woman; who's the wiser? We're not going to pick holes in each other's coats, I suppose?"

"No, indeed!" said Mrs. Dilber and the man together. "We should hope not."

"Very well, then!" cried the woman. "That's enough. Who's the worse for the loss of a few things like these? Not a dead man, I suppose."

"No, indeed," said Mrs. Dilber, laughing.

"If he wanted to keep 'em after he was dead, a wicked old screw," [15] pursued the woman, "why wasn't he natural in his lifetime? If he had been, he'd have had somebody to look after him when he was struck with Death, instead of lying gasping out his last there, alone by himself."

"It's the truest word that ever was spoke," said Mrs. Dilber. "It's a judgment on him." [16]

"I wish it was a little heavier one," [17] replied the woman; "and it should have been, you may depend upon it, if I could have laid my hands on anything else. Open that bundle, old Joe, and let me know the value of it. Speak out plain. I'm not afraid to be the

[14] "What odds then!" being an idiomatic expression that means "What's the difference?" or "What does it matter?"

[15] "Old screw" is slang for miser, cleverly echoed in the name Scrooge.

[16] Both women use the sinful behavior of the dead man to justify the sinful behavior of stealing from him—as Dickens dramatizes the old axiom "two wrongs do not make a right."

[17] While the first woman's use of *judgment* was at least sincere, the second woman uses the concept as a pun for her stolen articles, showing disregard for the judgment of either God or man.

[18] Lest we think, in Dickens's own judgment, there is only condemnation for such sinners, in *The Life of Our Lord* he wrote, "If they [the poor] are bad, think that they would have been better, if they had had kind friends, and good homes, and had been better taught. So, always try to make them better by kind persuading words; and always try to teach them and relieve them if you can."

[19] *Repent*, along with *judgment* and *sin*, is the third religious word used for sacrilegious actions, as Dickens continues his hellish parody.

first, nor afraid for them to see it. We know pretty well that we were helping ourselves, before we met here, I believe. It's no sin. [18] Open the bundle, Joe."

But the gallantry of her friends would not allow of this; and the man in faded black, mounting the breach first, produced his plunder. It was not extensive. A seal or two, a pencil-case, a pair of sleeve-buttons, and a brooch of no great value, were all. They were severally examined and appraised by old Joe, who chalked the sums he was disposed to give for each upon the wall, and added them up into a total when he found there was nothing more to come.

"That's your account," said Joe, "and I wouldn't give another sixpence, if I was to be boiled for not doing it. Who's next?"

Mrs. Dilber was next. Sheets and towels, a little wearing apparel, two old-fashioned silver teaspoons, a pair of sugar-tongs, and a few boots. Her account was stated on the wall in the same manner.

"I always give too much to ladies. It's a weakness of mine, and that's the way I ruin myself," said old Joe. "That's your account. If you asked me for another penny, and made it an open question, I'd repent [19] of being so liberal, and knock off half-a-crown."

"And now undo my bundle, Joe," said the first woman.

Joe went down on his knees for the greater convenience of opening it, and having unfastened a great many knots, dragged out a large and heavy roll of some dark stuff.

"What do you call this?" said Joe. "Bed-curtains!"

"Ah!" returned the woman, laughing and leaning forward on her crossed arms. "Bed-curtains!"

"You don't mean to say you took 'em down, rings and all, with him lying there?" said Joe.

"Yes I do," replied the woman. "Why not?"

"You were born to make your fortune," said Joe, "and you'll certainly do it."

"I certainly shan't hold my hand, when I can get anything in it by reaching it out, for the sake of such a man as He was, I promise you, Joe," returned the woman coolly. "Don't drop that oil upon the blankets, now."

"His blankets?" asked Joe.

"Whose else's do you think?" replied the woman. "He isn't likely to take cold without 'em, I dare say."

"I hope he didn't die of anything catching? Eh?" said old Joe, stopping in his work, and looking up.

"Don't you be afraid of that," returned the woman. "I an't so fond of his company that I'd loiter about him for such things, if he did. Ah! you may look through that shirt till your eyes ache; but you won't find a hole in it, nor a threadbare place. It's the best he had, and a fine one too. They'd have wasted it, if it hadn't been for me."

"What do you call wasting of it?" asked old Joe.

"Putting it on him to be buried in, to be sure," replied the woman with a laugh. "Somebody was fool enough to do it, but I took it off again. If calico an't good enough for such a purpose, it isn't good enough for anything. It's quite as becoming to the body. He can't look uglier than he did in that one."

Scrooge listened to this dialogue in horror. As they sat grouped about their spoil, in the scanty light afforded by the old man's lamp, he viewed them with a detestation and disgust, which could hardly have been greater, though they had been obscene demons, marketing the corpse itself.

"Ha, ha!" laughed the same woman, when old Joe, producing a flannel bag with money in it, told out their several gains upon the ground. "This is the end of it, you see! He frightened every one away from him when he was alive, to profit us when he was dead! Ha, ha, ha!"

"Spirit!" said Scrooge, shuddering from head to foot. "I see, I see. The case of this unhappy man might be my own. My life tends that way, now. Merciful Heaven, what is this!"

He recoiled in terror, for the scene had changed, and now he almost touched a bed: a bare, uncurtained bed: on which, beneath a ragged sheet, there lay a something covered up, which, though it was dumb, announced itself in awful language.

The room was very dark, too dark to be observed with any accuracy, though Scrooge glanced round it in obedience to a secret impulse, anxious to know what kind of room it was. A pale light, rising in the outer air, fell straight upon the bed; and on it, plundered and bereft, unwatched, unwept, uncared for, was the body of this man. [20]

Scrooge glanced towards the Phantom. Its steady hand was pointed to the head. The cover was so carelessly adjusted that the slightest raising of it, the motion of a finger upon Scrooge's part, would have disclosed the face. He thought of it, felt how easy it would be to do, and longed to do it; but had no more power to withdraw the veil than to dismiss the spectre at his side.

Oh cold, cold, rigid, dreadful Death, set up thine altar here, and dress it with such terrors as thou hast at thy command: for this is thy dominion! But of the loved, revered, and honoured head, thou canst not turn one hair to thy dread purposes, or make one feature odious. It is not that the hand is heavy and will fall down when released; it is not that the heart and pulse are still; but that the hand was open, generous, and true; [21] the heart brave, warm, and tender; and the pulse a man's. Strike, Shadow, strike! And see his

[20] In public readings, Dickens altered "this man" to "this plundered, unknown man," the identity of the dead man still being too awful to guess yet.

[21] Dickens suggests that the tragedy of a death is not simply in the loss of the life but the loss of any continued good deeds that life held.

good deeds [22] springing from the wound, to sow the world with life immortal!

No voice pronounced these words in Scrooge's ears, and yet he heard them when he looked upon the bed. He thought, if this man could be raised up now, what would be his foremost thoughts? Avarice, hard dealing, griping cares? They have brought him to a rich end, truly!

He lay, in the dark empty house, with not a man, a woman, or a child, to say that he was kind to me in this or that, and for the memory of one kind word I will be kind to him. A cat was tearing at the door, and there was a sound of gnawing rats beneath the hearth-stone. What *they* wanted in the room of death, and why they were so restless and disturbed, Scrooge did not dare to think.

"Spirit!" he said, "this is a fearful place. In leaving it, I shall not leave its lesson, trust me. Let us go!"

Still the Ghost pointed with an unmoved finger to the head.

"I understand you," Scrooge returned, "and I would do it, if I could. But I have not the power, Spirit. I have not the power."

Again it seemed to look upon him.

"If there is any person in the town, who feels emotion caused by this man's death," said Scrooge quite agonized, "show that person to me, Spirit, I beseech you!"

The Phantom spread its dark robe before him for a moment, like a wing; and withdrawing it, revealed a room by daylight, where a mother and her children were.

She was expecting some one, and with anxious eagerness; for she walked up and down the room; started at every sound; looked out from the window; glanced at the clock; tried, but in vain, to work with

[22] Dickens placed so much importance on godly good deeds, he instructed his children in his last will and testament to "humbly to try to guide themselves by the teaching of the New Testament in its broad spirit."

her needle; and could hardly bear the voices of the children in their play.

At length the long-expected knock was heard. She hurried to the door, and met her husband; a man whose face was care-worn and depressed, though he was young. There was a remarkable expression in it now; a kind of serious delight of which he felt ashamed, and which he struggled to repress.

He sat down to the dinner that had been hoarding for him by the fire; and when she asked him faintly what news (which was not until after a long silence), he appeared embarrassed how to answer.

"Is it good?" she said, "or bad?"—to help him.

"Bad," he answered.

"We are quite ruined?"

"No. There is hope yet, Caroline."

"If *he* relents," she said, amazed, "there is! Nothing is past hope, if such a miracle has happened."

"He is past relenting," said her husband. "He is dead."

She was a mild and patient creature if her face spoke truth; but she was thankful in her soul to hear it, and she said so, with clasped hands. She prayed forgiveness [23] the next moment, and was sorry; but the first was the emotion of her heart.

"What the half-drunken woman whom I told you of last night, said to me, when I tried to see him and obtain a week's delay; and what I thought was a mere excuse to avoid me; turns out to have been quite true. He was not only very ill, but dying, then."

"To whom will our debt be transferred?"

"I don't know. But before that time we shall be ready with the money; and even though we were not, [24] it would be a bad fortune indeed to find so merciless a creditor [25] in his successor. We may sleep to-night with light hearts, Caroline!"

[23] Unknowingly, this woman models for Scrooge the last step in his "reclamation"—he must pray for forgiveness to receive salvation.

[24] In sympathy with poor people such as these, Dickens wrote in *The Life of Our Lord*, "Heaven was made for them as well as for the rich, and God makes no difference between those who wear good clothes and those who go barefoot and in rags."

[25] Dickens had the "bad fortune" of knowing "so merciless a creditor," as his father was in and out of debt throughout Dickens's childhood, and at the lowest point, one creditor put his father in debtor's prison.

Yes. Soften it as they would, their hearts were lighter. The children's faces hushed, and clustered round to hear what they so little understood, were brighter; and it was a happier house for this man's death! The only emotion that the Ghost could show him, caused by the event, was one of pleasure.

"Let me see some tenderness connected with a death," said Scrooge; "or that dark chamber, Spirit, which we left just now, will be for ever present to me."

The Ghost conducted him through several streets familiar to his feet; and as they went along, Scrooge looked here and there to find himself, but nowhere was he to be seen. They entered poor Bob Cratchit's house; the dwelling he had visited before; and found the mother and the children seated round the fire.

Quiet. Very quiet. The noisy little Cratchits were as still as statues in one corner, and sat looking up at Peter, who had a book [26] before him. The mother and her daughters were engaged in sewing. But surely they were very quiet!

"'And He took a child, and set him in the midst of them.'" [27]

Where had Scrooge heard those words? He had not dreamed them. The boy must have read them out, as he and the Spirit crossed the threshold. Why did he not go on?

The mother laid her work upon the table, and put her hand up to her face.

"The colour hurts my eyes," she said.

The colour? Ah, poor Tiny Tim! [28]

"They're better now again," said Cratchit's wife. "It makes them weak by candle-light; and I wouldn't show weak eyes to your father when he comes home, for the world. It must be near his time."

[26] The Bible, actually.

[27] Dickens quotes Matthew 18:2 and Mark 9:36, both of which contain this passage, one of his personal favorites.

[28] Originally, the "colour" was "black," before Dickens marked it out. At the death of Tiny Tim, Mrs. Cratchit is sewing their mourning clothes.

"Past it rather," Peter answered, shutting up his book. "But I think he's walked a little slower than he used, these few last evenings, mother."

They were very quiet again. At last she said, and in a steady cheerful voice, that only faultered once:

"I have known him walk with—I have known him walk with Tiny Tim upon his shoulder, very fast indeed."

"And so have I," cried Peter. "Often."

"And so have I!" exclaimed another. So had all.

"But he was very light to carry," she resumed, intent upon her work, "and his father loved him so, that it was no trouble—no trouble. And there is your father at the door!"

She hurried out to meet him; and little Bob in his comforter—he had need of it, poor fellow—came in. His tea was ready for him on the hob, and they all tried who should help him to it most. Then the two young Cratchits got upon his knees and laid, each child a little cheek, against his face, as if they said, "Don't mind it, father. Don't be grieved!"

Bob was very cheerful with them, and spoke pleasantly to all the family. He looked at the work upon the table, and praised the industry and speed of Mrs. Cratchit and the girls. They would be done long before Sunday, he said.

"Sunday! [29] You went to-day, then, Robert?" said his wife.

"Yes, my dear," returned Bob. "I wish you could have gone. It would have done you good to see how green a place it is. But you'll see it often. I promised him that I would walk there on a Sunday. [30] My little, little child!" cried Bob. "My little child!" [31]

He broke down all at once. He couldn't help it. If he could have helped it, he and his child would have been farther apart perhaps than they were.

[29] Tiny Tim dies on Sunday, Christmas Day—as the birth of his Savior is celebrated.

[30] Bob promised Tiny Tim he would go to church each and every Sunday and walk in the churchyard (where the child would be buried)—just as they had so many times done together.

[31] The deaths of both a brother and a sister, which occurred when Dickens was a child (see Stave Three, Note 33), must have been on the adult author's mind when writing of the death of Tiny Tim.

He left the room, and went up stairs into the room above, which was lighted cheerfully, and hung with Christmas. [32] There was a chair set close beside the child, [33] and there were signs of some one having been there, lately. Poor Bob sat down in it, and when he had thought a little and composed himself, he kissed the little face. He was reconciled to what had happened, and went down again quite happy.

They drew about the fire, and talked; the girls and mother working still. Bob told them of the extraordinary kindness of Mr. Scrooge's nephew, whom he had scarcely seen but once, and who, meeting him in the street that day, and seeing that he looked a little—"just a little down you know" said Bob, enquired what had happened to distress him. "On which," said Bob, "for he is the pleasantest-spoken gentleman you ever heard, I told him. 'I am heartily sorry for it, Mr. Cratchit,' he said, 'and heartily sorry for your good wife.' By the bye, how he ever knew *that*, I don't know."

"Knew what, my dear?"

"Why, that you were a good wife," replied Bob.

"Everybody knows that!" said Peter.

"Very well observed, my boy!" cried Bob. "I hope they do. 'Heartily sorry,' he said, 'for your good wife. If I can be of service to you in any way,' he said, giving me his card, 'that's where I live. Pray come to me.' Now, it wasn't," cried Bob, "for the sake of anything he might be able to do for us, so much as for his kind way, that this was quite delightful. It really seemed as if he had known our Tiny Tim, [34] and felt with us."

"I'm sure he's a good soul!" said Mrs. Cratchit.

"You would be surer of it, my dear," returned Bob, "if you saw and spoke to him. I shouldn't be at all surprised, mark what I say, if he got Peter a better situation."

"Only hear that, Peter," said Mrs. Cratchit.

[32] In public readings, Dickens clarified "Christmas" with "Christmas holly," which symbolizes Christ (see Stave Three, Note 9).

[33] Here, but for the grace of God, went young Dickens, for the description by his friend John Forster of Dickens as a child—"he was a very little and very sickly boy, subject to attacks of violent spasm which disabled him from any active exertion"—would have fit Tiny Tim (*The Life of Charles Dickens*).

[34] Dickens first gave Tiny Tim the name "Little Fred," perhaps as a reference to both of his younger brothers, Frederick and Alfred. Alfred, like Tiny Tim, died in childhood.

"And then," cried one of the girls, "Peter will be keeping company with some one, and setting up for himself."

"Get along with you!" retorted Peter, grinning.

"It's just as likely as not," said Bob, "one of these days; though there's plenty of time for that, my dear. But however and whenever we part from one another, I am sure we shall none of us forget poor Tiny Tim—shall we—or this first parting that there was among us?"

"Never, father!" cried they all.

"And I know," said Bob, "I know, my dears, that when we recollect how patient and how mild he was; although he was a little, little child; we shall not quarrel easily among ourselves, and forget poor Tiny Tim in doing it." [35]

"No, never, father!" they all cried again.

"I am very happy," said little Bob, "I am very happy!"

Mrs. Cratchit kissed him, his daughters kissed him, the two young Cratchits kissed him, and Peter and himself shook hands. Spirit of Tiny Tim, thy childish essence was from God! [36]

"Spectre," said Scrooge, "something informs me that our parting moment is at hand. I know it, but I know not how. Tell me what man that was whom we saw lying dead?"

The Ghost of Christmas Yet To Come conveyed him, as before—though at a different time, he thought: indeed, there seemed no order in these latter visions, save that they were in the Future—into the resorts of business men, but showed him not himself. Indeed, the Spirit did not stay for anything, but went straight on, as to the end just now desired, until besought by Scrooge to tarry for a moment.

"This court," said Scrooge, "through which we

[35] In comparing Tiny Tim to the Christ child, modern author Michael Patrick Hearn wrote, "The Ghosts of Christmas Past, Present and Yet To Come are the new Wise Men. And just as these [biblical] kings were led to a poor abode, Scrooge makes a pilgrimage to the humble home of Tiny Tim" (*The Annotated Christmas Carol*).

[36] "Thy childish essence was from God" and, at one time, God was a childish essence. As Dickens said of Jesus in a speech at a children's hospital, Christ was "the universal embodiment of all mercy and compassion.... Him who was once a child himself, and a poor one."

hurry now, is where my place of occupation is, and has been for a length of time. I see the house. Let me behold what I shall be, in days to come."

The Spirit stopped; the hand was pointed elsewhere.

"The house is yonder," Scrooge exclaimed. "Why do you point away?"

The inexorable finger underwent no change.

Scrooge hastened to the window of his office, and looked in. It was an office still, but not his. The furniture was not the same, and the figure in the chair was not himself. The Phantom pointed as before.

He joined it once again, and wondering why and whither he had gone, accompanied it until they reached an iron gate. He paused to look round before entering.

A churchyard. [37] Here, then, the wretched man whose name he had now to learn, lay underneath the ground. It was a worthy place. Walled in by houses; overrun by grass and weeds, the growth of vegetation's death, not life; choked up with too much burying; fat with repleted appetite. A worthy place!

The Spirit stood among the graves, and pointed down to One. He advanced towards it trembling. The Phantom was exactly as it had been, but he dreaded that he saw new meaning in its solemn shape.

"Before I draw nearer to that stone to which you point," said Scrooge, "answer me one question. Are these the shadows of the things that Will be, or are they shadows of things that May be, only?"

Still the Ghost pointed downward to the grave by which it stood.

"Men's courses will foreshadow certain ends, to which, if persevered in, they must lead," said Scrooge. "But if the courses be departed from, the ends will change. Say it is thus with what you show me!"

[37] The fifth church Dickens mentions is thought to be All Hallows Staining (Gwen Major, "Scrooge's Chambers").

[38] At the time of his death, Dickens was so closely linked to the celebration of Christmas that one young girl was reported to have said, "Dickens dead? Then will Father Christmas die too?"

[39] Dickens again indicates that there is a power higher than the Spirits (see Stave One, Note 52) as this Spirit "intercedes" for Scrooge, recalling how the Holy Spirit intercedes for us, as in Romans 8:26, 27.

[40] Dickens describes the hand as "kind"—and for the first time, gives this mysterious Spirit a human, or even heavenly, quality.

[41] The trinity of Spirits in Scrooge reflects the Holy Spirit (one of the Trinity) in us.

[42] Scrooge again recalls Jacob wrestling with a spirit from Genesis 32 (see Stave Two, Note 50).

[43] The moment of Scrooge's prayer is the moment of his salvation—as he held up "his hands in one last prayer," the Phantom "shrunk, collapsed, and dwindled."

[44] For Christian readers who interpret Scrooge's visitations as a dream, this seems the third most obvious indication (see Stave Two, Note 9 and Stave Two, Note 52). The "tall and stately" Spirit appears to revert back to Scrooge's bedpost.

The Spirit was immovable as ever.

Scrooge crept towards it, trembling as he went; and following the finger, read upon the stone of the neglected grave his own name, EBENEZER SCROOGE. [38]

"Am *I* that man who lay upon the bed?" he cried, upon his knees.

The finger pointed from the grave to him, and back again.

"No, Spirit! Oh no, no!"

The finger still was there.

"Spirit!" he cried, tight clutching at its robe, "hear me! I am not the man I was. I will not be the man I must have been but for this intercourse. Why show me this, if I am past all hope!"

For the first time the hand appeared to shake.

"Good Spirit," he pursued, as down upon the ground he fell before it: "Your nature intercedes [39] for me, and pities me. Assure me that I yet may change these shadows you have shown me, by an altered life!"

The kind hand trembled. [40]

"I will honour Christmas in my heart, and try to keep it all the year. I will live in the Past, the Present, and the Future. The Spirits of all Three shall strive within me. [41] I will not shut out the lessons that they teach. Oh, tell me I may sponge away the writing on this stone!"

In his agony, he caught the spectral hand. It sought to free itself, but he was strong in his entreaty, and detained it. [42] The Spirit, stronger yet, repulsed him.

Holding up his hands in one last prayer [43] to have his fate reversed, he saw an alteration in the Phantom's hood and dress.

It shrunk, collapsed, and dwindled down into a bedpost. [44]

Salvation

I. TELLING THE STORY

Stave Four leads Scrooge toward salvation as the Ghost of Christmas Yet To Come foretells not one but two deaths. While the first death is of an unloved man, the second death is of a beloved child. And though Scrooge is saddened to see the demise of Tiny Tim, he is distraught to witness the death that no one mourns because of the life he never fully lived. Through our study of this chapter, we'll examine what Scrooge learns about his life through glimpsing his death and find out what this reveals about the source of our salvation.

Key Verse

"Whoever believes in the Son has eternal life, but whoever rejects the Son will not see life, for God's wrath remains on him."
—JOHN 3:36

A. As Scrooge walked with the Spirit through familiar streets, he kept looking for himself. What does this tell us about Scrooge's thinking? Did he believe he could be saved?

B. Describe the differences between Scrooge's death and the death of Tiny Tim. What lesson does Bob Cratchit tell his family they can learn from remembering Tiny Tim's life? What lesson does the charwoman give us from Scrooge's life?

ℭ. What do you think Scrooge fears more—his lonely death or his wasted life? Explain your reasons for your answer.

𝔇. When Scrooge finds himself suddenly in the room of the dead man, he is frightened and cries out "Merciful Heaven, what is this!" How might the visions Scrooge is given of his future life (or death) actually be acts of mercy toward him?

II. TELLING YOUR STORY

We look for salvation everywhere. But it can't be found in money, knowledge, or power. Our Lord Jesus Christ came to offer salvation to all people—through him alone. Christ did not come simply to encourage us to become better people or to help us learn how to save ourselves. He came to save us from death by sin through the salvation that leads to eternal life.

𝔎𝔢𝔶 𝔙𝔢𝔯𝔰𝔢

"Salvation is found in no one else, for there is no other name under heaven given to men by which we must be saved."
—ACTS 4:12

𝔄. Have you ever been in trouble and had to call for help? When did you call? Whom did you call? How did it feel to be rescued?

𝔅. What does being saved by Jesus mean to you?

ℭ. Scrooge seemed to want to save his own life through his actions. Have you ever tried to achieve a kind of salvation through your own power? Have you ever tried to fix the consequences of your sin? Describe these situations.

𝕯. Like Scrooge, many of us have to be brought to a point of despair before we realize that our hope is in Jesus. At what point in your life did you realize that you needed salvation?

III. TELLING THE STORY OF CHRISTMAS

It could be said that the three Spirits who visited with Scrooge came bearing gifts for him—gifts of memory, knowledge, and sight. Their actions pointed to the true source of Christmas peace, joy, and hope. In this, they were not unlike the wise men of the Christmas story, who also came bearing gifts and followed the way to Christ (Matthew 3:1-12).

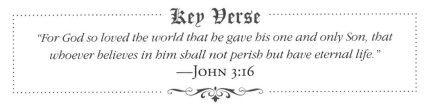

Key Verse

"For God so loved the world that he gave his one and only Son, that whoever believes in him shall not perish but have eternal life."
—JOHN 3:16

𝕬. What is the most precious gift you have ever given away? How did you feel about giving it?

𝕭. The wise men followed a star and traveled a long way to find the new King. What do you do to learn more about Christ?

𝕮. What does having the gift of eternal life mean to you? How does it affect how you live?

𝕯. The gifts the wise men offered to Christ were appropriate for who he was, and who he was going to be. They were costly gifts, fit for a king. They also foreshadowed his death, being items that were used in burial rituals. What kind of gifts can you offer to Jesus?

IV. Living the Story

It is comforting to realize that we do not have to become perfect before we can receive God's gift. But at the same time, it is difficult for us to understand that there is nothing we need to do or can do to save ourselves. Perhaps this is why Dickens includes this verse in this stave: "And He took a child, and set him in the midst of them." To receive the gift of salvation, we have to let go of control and become like children, fully dependent on our Father, and wholeheartedly believing in him.

Ask God to help you give thanks for the gift of salvation by:

✦ Remembering that only Jesus can save you.

✦ Giving glory to God in all that you do.

✦ Offering the gift of salvation to others by telling them about Christ.

For Further Study

Psalm 13

Isaiah 30:15, 16

Luke 18:22

John 3:16-21

Acts 16:30-34

2 Corinthians 6:1, 2

Ephesians 1:11-14; 2:1-10

1 Thessalonians 5:4-11

1 Timothy 1:15-17

Titus 2:11-14; 3:3-5

The End of It

Yes! and the bedpost was his own. [1] The bed was his own, the room was his own. Best and happiest of all, the Time before him was his own, to make amends in!

"I will live in the Past, the Present, and the Future!" Scrooge repeated, as he scrambled out of bed. "The Spirits of all Three shall strive within me. Oh Jacob Marley! Heaven, and the Christmas Time be praised for this! I say it on my knees, old Jacob; on my knees!" [2]

He was so fluttered and so glowing with his good intentions, that his broken voice would scarcely answer to his call. He had been sobbing violently in his conflict with the Spirit, and his face was wet with tears.

"They are not torn down," cried Scrooge, folding one of his bed-curtains in his arms, "they are not torn down, rings and all. They are here: I am here: the shadows of the things that would have been, may be dispelled. They will be. I know they will!"

His hands were busy with his garments all this time: turning them inside out, putting them on

[1] Some literal-minded Christians prefer the dream interpretation because they suggest Luke 16:19-31 indicates the dead cannot return to warn us (as Marley does); Ecclesiastes 7:14 states man cannot know the future (as the third Spirit reveals); and the "Spirits" are not identified as "angels." Others may point to 1 Samuel 28 as evidence that communication with spiritual beings can occur. However, many simply read *Carol* as a moral allegory, without a literal interpretation.

[2] Dickens really believed in the redemption of those like Scrooge, as he wrote in *The Life of Our Lord*: "people who have been wicked . . . and who are truly sorry for it, however late in their lives, and pray God to forgive them, will be forgiven and will go to Heaven too."

upside down, tearing them, mislaying them, making them parties to every kind of extravagance.

"I don't know what to do!" cried Scrooge, laughing and crying in the same breath; and making a perfect Laocoön [3] of himself with his stockings. "I am as light as a feather, I am as happy as an angel, I am as merry as a school-boy. I am as giddy as a drunken man. A merry Christmas to everybody! A happy New Year to all the world. Hallo here! Whoop! Hallo!"

He had frisked into the sitting-room, and was now standing there: perfectly winded.

"There's the saucepan that the gruel was in!" cried Scrooge, starting off again, and frisking round the fire-place. "There's the door, by which the Ghost of Jacob Marley entered! There's the corner where the Ghost of Christmas Present, sat! There's the window where I saw the wandering Spirits! It's all right, it's all true, it all happened. Ha ha ha!"

Really, for a man who had been out of practice for so many years, it was a splendid laugh, a most illustrious laugh. The father of a long, long, line of brilliant laughs!

"I don't know what day of the month it is!" said Scrooge. "I don't know how long I've been among the Spirits. I don't know anything. I'm quite a baby. [4] Never mind. I don't care. I'd rather be a baby. Hallo! Whoop! Hallo here!"

He was checked in his transports by the churches ringing out the lustiest peals he had ever heard. [5] Clash, clang, hammer, ding, dong, bell. Bell, dong, ding; hammer, clang, clash! Oh, glorious, glorious!

Running to the window, he opened it, and put out his head. No fog, no mist; clear, bright, jovial, stirring, cold; cold, piping for the blood to dance to; Golden sunlight; Heavenly sky; sweet fresh air; merry bells. Oh, glorious. Glorious!

[3] Dickens is referring to Virgil's story in *The Aeneid* of a Trojan priest who suffered the wrath of the goddess Athena and was strangled by serpents, along with his two sons.

[4] By becoming "quite a baby," Scrooge fulfills one of Dickens's favorite Bible passages (see Stave Four, Note 27)—Matthew 18:2, 3 (*KJV*): "And Jesus called a little child unto him, and set him in the midst of them, and said, 'Verily I say unto you, except ye be converted, and become as little children, ye shall not enter into the kingdom of heaven.'"

[5] Scrooge does not "know what to do"—until he hears the church bells.

"What's to-day?" cried Scrooge, calling downward to a boy in Sunday clothes, who perhaps had loitered in to look about him.

"Eh?" returned the boy, with all his might of wonder.

"What's to-day, my fine fellow?" said Scrooge.

"To-day!" replied the boy. "Why, CHRISTMAS DAY."

"It's Christmas Day!" said Scrooge to himself. "I haven't missed it. The Spirits have done it all in one night. They can do anything they like. Of course they can. Of course they can. Hallo, my fine fellow!"

"Hallo!" returned the boy.

"Do you know the Poulterer's, in the next street but one, at the corner?" Scrooge inquired.

"I should hope I did," replied the lad.

"An intelligent boy!" said Scrooge. "A remarkable boy! Do you know whether they've sold the prize Turkey that was hanging up there? Not the little prize Turkey: the big one?"

"What, the one as big as me?" returned the boy.

"What a delightful boy!" said Scrooge. "It's a pleasure to talk to him. Yes, my buck!"

"It's hanging there now," replied the boy.

"Is it?" said Scrooge. "Go and buy it."

"Walk-ER!" [6] exclaimed the boy.

"No, no," said Scrooge, "I am in earnest. Go and buy it, and tell 'em to bring it here, that I may give them the direction where to take it. Come back with the man, and I'll give you a shilling. Come back with him in less than five minutes, and I'll give you half-a-crown!"

The boy was off like a shot. He must have had a steady hand at a trigger who could have got a shot off half so fast.

"I'll send it to Bob Cratchit's!" [7] whispered Scrooge, rubbing his hands, and splitting with a

[6] "Walk-ER!" is a Cockney slang term used to express disbelief. When Dickens would read this line he would put "his thumb to his nose, and spread out his fingers, with a jeer, at the syllable ER. This was a common way to call their pals 'fools' without using the word" (from Philip Collins, *A Christmas Carol: The Public Reading Version*).

[7] When an economic conservative criticized Scrooge's generosity in the *Westminster Review*, asking who went without turkey so that Bob Cratchit could have his, Dickens deflated his critic with a quip to a friend, writing that "the *Westminster Review* considered Scrooge's presentation of the turkey to Bob Cratchit as grossly incompatible with political economy."

[8] Joe Miller was a popular comic actor whose sayings were collected and published as *Joe Miller's Jests* by the dramatist John Mottley. Though the book became popular as a collection of English wit, apparently the man himself was not actually very funny and much of what was in the book, if not all, was not original to him.

[9] Seemingly, the knocker has an "honest expression" because Marley (whose face appeared in the knocker) told the Truth—and now Scrooge knows it too.

[10] The effect of this passage on readers was nearly evangelical—as was noted in *Wilkes's Spirit of the Times* in 1867 (over twenty years after *Carol* was published!): "Everybody who reads it and who has money immediately rushes off and buys a turkey for the poor."

laugh. "He sha'n't know who sends it. It's twice the size of Tiny Tim. Joe Miller [8] never made such a joke as sending it to Bob's will be!"

The hand in which he wrote the address was not a steady one, but write it he did, somehow, and went down stairs to open the street door, ready for the coming of the poulterer's man. As he stood there, waiting his arrival, the knocker caught his eye.

"I shall love it, as long as I live!" cried Scrooge, patting it with his hand. "I scarcely ever looked at it before. What an honest expression [9] it has in its face! It's a wonderful knocker!—Here's the Turkey! Hallo! Whoop! How are you! Merry Christmas!"

It *was* a Turkey! [10] He never could have stood upon his legs, that bird. He would have snapped 'em short off in a minute, like sticks of sealing-wax.

"Why, it's impossible to carry that to Camden Town," said Scrooge. "You must have a cab."

The chuckle with which he said this, and the chuckle with which he paid for the Turkey, and the chuckle with which he paid for the cab, and the chuckle with which he recompensed the boy, were only to be exceeded by the chuckle with which he sat down breathless in his chair again, and chuckled till he cried.

Shaving was not an easy task, for his hand continued to shake very much; and shaving requires attention, even when you don't dance while you are at it. But if he had cut the end of his nose off, he would have put a piece of sticking-plaister over it, and been quite satisfied.

He dressed himself "all in his best," and at last got out into the streets. The people were by this time pouring forth, as he had seen them with the Ghost of Christmas Present; and walking with his hands behind him, Scrooge regarded every one with a delighted smile. He looked so irresistibly pleasant, in a word, that three or four good-humoured fellows said, "Good morning, sir! A merry Christmas to you!" And Scrooge said often afterwards, that of all the blithe sounds he had ever heard, those were the blithest in his ears.

He had not gone far, when coming on towards him he beheld the portly gentleman, who had walked into his counting-house the day before and said, "Scrooge and Marley's, I believe?" It sent a pang across his heart to think how this old gentleman would look upon him when they met; but he knew what path lay straight before him, and he took it. [11]

"My dear sir," said Scrooge, quickening his pace, and taking the old gentleman by both his hands. "How do you do? I hope you succeeded yesterday. It was very kind of you. A merry Christmas to you, sir!"

"Mr. Scrooge?"

"Yes," said Scrooge. "That is my name, and I fear it may not be pleasant to you. Allow me to ask your pardon. And will you have the goodness"—here Scrooge whispered in his ear.

"Lord bless me!" cried the gentleman, as if his breath were gone. "My dear Mr. Scrooge, are you serious?"

"If you please," said Scrooge. "Not a farthing less. A great many back-payments are included in it, I assure you. [12] Will you do me that favour?"

"My dear sir," said the other, shaking hands with him. "I don't know what to say to such munifi—"

"Don't say anything, please," retorted Scrooge. "Come and see me. Will you come and see me?"

"I will!" cried the old gentleman. And it was clear he meant to do it.

"Thank'ee," said Scrooge. "I am much obliged to you. I thank you fifty times. Bless you!"

[11] As Dickens cared so much about godly good deeds (see Stave Four, Note 22), he has Scrooge set an example for the reader by putting his goodwill to good work.

[12] Dickens knew that, for a man like Scrooge, and men like him in the readership, a monetary contribution gives the most convincing evidence of his rehabilitation and confidence in his salvation.

He went to church, and walked about the streets, and watched the people hurrying to and fro, and patted children on the head, and questioned beggars, and looked down into the kitchens of houses, and up to the windows, and found that everything could yield him pleasure. He had never dreamed that any walk—that anything—could give him so much happiness. In the afternoon, he turned his steps towards his nephew's house.

He passed the door a dozen times, before he had the courage to go up and knock. But he made a dash, and did it:

"Is your master at home, my dear?" said Scrooge to the girl. Nice girl! Very.

"Yes, sir."

"Where is he, my love?" said Scrooge.

"He's in the dining-room, sir, along with mistress. I'll show you up stairs, if you please."

"Thank'ee. He knows me," said Scrooge, with his hand already on the dining-room lock. "I'll go in here, my dear."

He turned it gently, and sidled his face in, round the door. They were looking at the table (which was spread out in great array); for these young housekeepers are always nervous on such points, and like to see that everything is right.

"Fred!" said Scrooge. [13]

Dear heart alive, how his niece by marriage started! Scrooge had forgotten, for the moment, about her sitting in the corner with the footstool, or he wouldn't have done it, on any account.

"Why bless my soul!" cried Fred, "who's that?"

"It's I. Your uncle Scrooge. I have come to dinner. Will you let me in, Fred?"

Let him in! It is a mercy he didn't shake his arm off. He was at home in five minutes. Nothing could

[13] Here, Scrooge the changed man seems changed into Fred—as he enters the room full of the same hearty goodwill that Fred modeled earlier when he visited Scrooge, even having a similar startling effect on those already present.

be heartier. His niece looked just the same. So did Topper when *he* came. So did the plump sister, when *she* came. So did every one when *they* came. Wonderful party, wonderful games, wonderful unanimity, won-der-ful happiness! [14]

But he was early at the office next morning. [15] Oh he was early there. If he could only be there first, and catch Bob Cratchit coming late! That was the thing he had set his heart upon.

And he did it; yes he did! The clock struck nine. No Bob. A quarter past. No Bob. He was full eighteen minutes and a half, behind his time. Scrooge sat with his door wide open, that he might see him come into the Tank.

His hat was off, before he opened the door; his comforter too. He was on his stool in a jiffy; driving away with his pen, as if he were trying to overtake nine o'clock.

"Hallo!" growled Scrooge, in his accustomed voice as near as he could feign it. "What do you mean by coming here at this time of day?"

"I am very sorry, sir," said Bob. "I *am* behind my time."

"You are?" repeated Scrooge. "Yes. I think you are. Step this way, if you please."

"It's only once a year, sir," pleaded Bob, appearing from the Tank. "It shall not be repeated. I was making rather merry yesterday, sir."

"Now, I'll tell you what, my friend," said Scrooge, "I am not going to stand this sort of thing any longer. And therefore," he continued, leaping from his stool, and giving Bob such a dig in the waistcoat that he staggered back into the Tank again: "and therefore I am about to raise your salary!"

Bob trembled, and got a little nearer to the ruler. He had a momentary idea of knocking Scrooge

[14] This is the night Scrooge had seen with the Spirit of Christmas Present, and yet the former miser has in fact changed the future with his presence — a quiet statement on how much power is in such a simple thing as being there.

[15] In England, the next morning was celebrated as Saint Stephen's Day or Boxing Day, a day when an employer kindly rewarded his worker with a box of gifts. In accordance with the spirit of that day, Dickens has Scrooge raise Bob's salary.

[16] Dickens nearly left out one of the most uplifting sentences in *Carol*, adding before printing that Tiny Tim did not die—giving the impression that it was the new Scrooge who saved the child.

[17] In public readings, Dickens added, "in that respect"—while he did not walk with Spirits, it is assumed Scrooge still prayed to God.

[18] The *Total Abstinence Principle* is a pun—referring to Scrooge abstaining from Spirits and to the Temperance ideal of abstention from alcoholic spirits. Dickens was criticized for his mentions of such drinks. However, he believed drinking was harmless in moderation. As James Fields noted in *Yesterdays with Authors*: "When the punch was ready, he drank less of it than any one who might be present. It was the *sentiment* of the thing, and not the thing itself, that engaged his attention."

[19] Dickens wishes his reader God's blessing—which he surely hoped *Carol* was.

[20] Twelve years after *Carol*'s publication, Dickens wrote to a friend an epilogue of sorts: "Scrooge is delighted to find that Bob Cratchit is enjoying his holiday in such a delightful situation; and he says (with that warmth of that nature which has distinguished him since his conversion) 'Make the most of it, Bob; make the most of it!'"

down with it; holding him; and calling to the people in the court for help and a strait-waistcoat.

"A merry Christmas, Bob!" said Scrooge, with an earnestness that could not be mistaken, as he clapped him on the back. "A merrier Christmas, Bob, my good fellow, than I have given you, for many a year! I'll raise your salary, and endeavour to assist your struggling family, and we will discuss your affairs this very afternoon, over a Christmas bowl of smoking bishop, Bob! Make up the fires, and buy another coal-scuttle before you dot another i, Bob Cratchit!"

Scrooge was better than his word. He did it all, and infinitely more; and to Tiny Tim, who did NOT die, [16] he was a second father. He became as good a friend, as good a master, and as good a man, as the good old city knew, or any other good old city, town, or borough, in the good old world. Some people laughed to see the alteration in him, but he let them laugh, and little heeded them; for he was wise enough to know that nothing ever happened on this globe, for good, at which some people did not have their fill of laughter in the outset; and knowing that such as these would be blind anyway, he thought it quite as well that they should wrinkle up their eyes in grins, as have the malady in less attractive forms. His own heart laughed: and that was quite enough for him.

He had no further intercourse with Spirits, [17] but lived upon the Total Abstinence Principle, [18] ever afterwards; and it was always said of him, that he knew how to keep Christmas well, if any man alive possessed the knowledge. May that be truly said of us, and all of us! And so, as Tiny Tim observed, God bless Us, Every One! [19]

THE END. [20]

Rebirth

I. TELLING THE STORY

Stave Five is titled "The End of It," but it really marks a beginning for Ebenezer Scrooge. After facing his death, he is reborn into a new life, and he embraces it as you might expect anyone would who has been given a second chance at living. Through his actions we can see how the everlasting privilege of eternal life gives a freedom that no amount of money can buy.

Key Verse

"Let's have a feast and celebrate. For this son of mine was dead and is alive again; he was lost and is found."
—LUKE 15:23, 24

A. We often hear people say about giving gifts that "it's the thought that counts." However, in Scrooge's case, why was it important for him to celebrate his new life by giving large, generous gifts?

B. To what character does Scrooge not give any money? What does he give instead, and why is this meaningful?

C. Compare the way Scrooge walks through the streets with the first time he walked through the streets. What is different? What is the same? What has changed about Ebenezer, and what has changed about the people around him?

Jesus said, "I have come that they may have life, and have it to the full" (John 10:10). How was Scrooge's life before he met the Spirits empty? With what activities or people does he start filling his life up in Stave Five?

II. TELLING YOUR STORY

When we accept Jesus as our Savior, we receive the Holy Spirit, who helps us to know and follow God's will. In this state, we are freed from living as slaves to sin. For most of us, our new lives in Christ will not be marked by the kinds of dramatic changes that happened to Scrooge: constant frowns to constant laughter, having no kind words to overflowing with kindness. But people should be able to see something different about us if we are living our lives for God.

Key Verse

"You were taught, with regard to your former way of life, to put off your old self, which is being corrupted by its deceitful desires; to be made new in the attitude of your minds; and to put on the new self, created to be like God in true righteousness and holiness."
—EPHESIANS 4:22-24

𝕬. Have you ever woken up and felt like Scrooge did when he opened the window to the clear, bright day? Have you ever woken up hating the new day? When you are feeling grumpy, what can you do to change your attitude?

𝕭. As Scrooge went to church and walked about, he "found that everything could yield him pleasure." Paul says in 1 Thessalonians 5:16 to "Be joyful always." How can knowing Jesus help us to find joy in all kinds of situations?

𝕮. Scrooge describes himself as being "as light as a feather . . . as happy as an angel . . . as merry as a school-boy . . . as giddy as a drunken man." Often when we first come to know and accept Christ we feel very happy and free. Why is it difficult to maintain that feeling?

𝕯. "Some people laughed to see the alteration" in Scrooge. Fearing what people might think about them is often a big stumbling block to those who want to make a change in their lives. What makes it hard for you to change? What makes it easy for you to fall back into the way of your old self?

III. Telling the Story of Christmas

Dickens wrote that "it is good to be children sometimes, and never better than at Christmas, when its mighty Founder was a child himself" (Stave Three). Though the world sometimes finds it hard to remember, there would be no Christmas without the Christ child. Christ came to the world to reveal to us the great promise of God: that death does not have to be the end, but the beginning of a new life with God. As we celebrate the birth of Jesus, let us also renew our commitment to live as children of God.

Key Verse

"Be imitators of God, therefore, as dearly loved children and live a life of love, just as Christ loved us and gave himself up for us as a fragrant offering and a sacrifice to God."
—Ephesians 5:1, 2

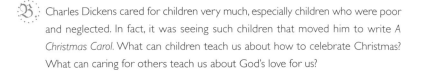

𝕬. How have you put the birth of Christ in the center of your Christmas celebrations? If you haven't done this, what are some things you could do to make Christ the center?

𝕭. Charles Dickens cared for children very much, especially children who were poor and neglected. In fact, it was seeing such children that moved him to write *A Christmas Carol*. What can children teach us about how to celebrate Christmas? What can caring for others teach us about God's love for us?

𝕮. When Joseph and Mary brought the infant Jesus to the temple, the man named Simeon said to Mary, "This child is destined to cause the falling and rising of many in Israel, and to be a sign that will be spoken against, so that the thoughts of many hearts will be revealed" (Luke 2:34). What does the way you celebrate Christmas reveal about what you believe? How does what you say and do throughout the year reflect your faith in Christ?

𝕯. Messages of love, giving, peace, and joy are everywhere at Christmastime. It's a good time to examine our hearts and see how we can better live lives of love as children of God. What does it mean to be a child of God? What do we need to sacrifice to love others with the love of Christ?

IV. LIVING THE STORY

Though *A Christmas Carol* is just a fictional story about an imaginary man, reading it can help us understand something about the true message of the real man and Son of God, Jesus Christ. Jesus came to earth to save his people from their sins. He came not just for that one time, or for only at Christmastime, but for all time. If we believe in Christ, we need to honor Christmas in our hearts and "try to keep it all the year." Perhaps then it will be said of us not just that we "knew how to keep Christmas well," but that we knew Christ well.

Ask God to help you keep Christmas in your heart by:

✦ Strengthening your feelings of compassion for others.

✦ Helping you find joy in all circumstances.

✦ Committing each day to live as a child of God.

For Further Study

Psalm 51
Luke 15:11-24
John 1:10-14
Romans 5; 8:1-17
Ephesians 5:8-21
Galatians 5:22, 23
1 Thessalonians 4:7, 8; 5:12-18
1 John 2:1-6
Hebrews 9:27, 28

The tale of Ebenezer Scrooge has been performed, printed, and portrayed in thousands of ways since its first 1843 printing, even including a graphic novel version and a Nintendo DS game version (to go with Disney's newest film offering). What follows is a limited selection of resources suggested for use with your family or group, either for learning more about the Charles Dickens classic or just for enjoying it in a different format.

Editions of *A Christmas Carol*

The Annotated Christmas Carol, edited with an introduction and notes by Michael Patrick Hearn (New York: W. W. Norton & Company, Inc., 2004). A thoroughly researched edition including black-and-white illustrations by John Leech, the original illustrator of the 1843 edition.

A Christmas Carol, illus. by P. J. Lynch (Candlewick, 2006). A richly illustrated edition.

A Christmas Carol: A Young Reader's Edition of the Classic Holiday Tale, illus. by Christian Birmingham (Philadephia: Running Press Kids, 2000). Recommended for ages 9-12.

Books about Charles Dickens

Charles Dickens, by G. K. Chesterton (London: Methuen & Co, 1906).

Dickens, by Peter Ackroyd (New York: HarperCollins, 1990).

The Life of Charles Dickens, by John Forster (London: Chapman and Hall, 1872–1874).

The Man Who Invented Christmas, by Les Standiford (New York: Crown Publishers, 2008).

Books to help you create a Dickensian Christmas

Dickens' Christmas: A Victorian Celebration, by Simon Callow (New York: Harry N. Abrams, 2003). Includes text of some of Dickens's Christmas writings as well as authentic recipes and music from the early nineteenth century.

What Jane Austen Ate and Charles Dickens Knew: From Fox Hunting to Whist—The Facts of Daily Life in Nineteenth-Century England, by David Pool (New York: Touchstone, 1994). The title says it all.

Films based on *A Christmas Carol* (in order of year of release)
Scrooge (1951), starring Alastair Sim as Scrooge, released as *A Christmas Carol* in the U.S., and directed by Brian Desmond Hurst.

Scrooge (1970), a musical film adaptation starring Albert Finney as Scrooge, directed by Ronald Neame.

A Christmas Carol (1971), an award-winning animated short film with Alastair Sim as the voice of Scrooge, directed by Richard Williams.

Mickey's Christmas Carol (1983), an animated short film featuring various Walt Disney characters and starring Scrooge McDuck, directed by Burny Mattinson.

A Christmas Carol (1984), a television movie adaptation starring George C. Scott as Scrooge, directed by Clive Donner.

A Christmas Carol (1999), a television movie adaptation with Patrick Stewart as Scrooge, directed by David Hugh Jones.

Disney's A Christmas Carol (2009), a motion capture animated film directed by Robert Zemeckis, with Jim Carrey portraying all the phases of Scrooge and the three Spirits.

Audio recordings of *A Christmas Carol*
A Christmas Carol, read by British actor Jim Dale, an unabridged edition available on CD.

A Christmas Carol, performed by Jonathan Winters, the holiday favorite from National Public Radio, available on CD.

~⚬⚬ BIBLIOGRAPHY ⚬⚬~

Information about definitions and etymology of words used in the 1843 edition comes mainly from The Oxford English Dictionary *online edition (www.oed.com), published by the Oxford University Press.*

Information about Charles Dickens and A Christmas Carol *was gathered from the following sources.*

Bent, Samuel Arthur. *Short Sayings of Great Men*. Boston: James R. Osgood and Company, 1882.

Chancellor, E. Beresford. *The London of Charles Dickens*. New York: George H. Doran Company, 1924.

Dickens, Charles. *The Annotated Christmas Carol*. With an introduction and notes by Michael Patrick Hearn. New York: W. W. Norton & Company, Inc., 2004.

Dickens, Charles. *A Christmas Carol: The Public Reading Version*. Edited and with introduction by Philip Collins. New York: The New York Public Library, 1971.

Dickens, Charles. *Christmas Books*. London: Chapman and Hall, 1852.

Dickens, Charles. "Gone Astray." *Household Words*, August 31, 1853.

Dickens, Charles. *The Life of Our Lord*. London: Associated Newspapers, 1934.

Dickens, Mamie. *My Father As I Recall Him*. London: The Roxburghe Press, 1896.

Fields, James T. *Yesterdays with Authors*. London: Sampson Low, Marston, Low, and Searle, 1872.

Forster, John. *The Life of Charles Dickens*. London: Chapman and Hall, 1872–1874.

Johnson, Frank S. "About 'A Christmas Carol.'" *The Dickensian*, Winter, 1932–33.

Kent, Charles. *Charles Dickens as a Reader*. London: Chapman and Hall, 1872.

Major, Gwen. "Scrooge's Chambers." *The Dickensian*, Winter, 1932–33.

Standiford, Les. *The Man Who Invented Christmas: How Charles Dickens's* A Christmas Carol *Rescued His Career and Revived Our Holiday Spirits*. New York: Crown Publishers, 2008.

Walder, Dennis. *Dickens and Religion*. New York: HarperCollins, 1981.

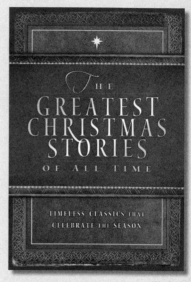